REINTRODUCTION

Want More
Do More
Be More

Emanuel Jones

ISBN 978-1-63961-933-7 (paperback)
ISBN 978-1-63961-934-4 (digital)

Christian Faith Publishing, Inc.
832 Park Avenue
Meadville, PA 16335
www.christianfaithpublishing.com

Printed in the United States of America

To my family, friends, associates, believers,
buyers, readers, and journey supporters.
Above all to GOD and the kingdom of GOD.

CONTENTS

Preface...7

Acknowledgments 9

Introduction...11

Chapter 1: Acknowledge You Can Do Better 13

Chapter 2: Prayer Will Bring You Out 16

Chapter 3: Thinking Greatness...22

Chapter 4: Making Room in a Crowded Place.........................26

Chapter 5: Open Opportunity..31

Chapter 6: Bridge the Gap...35

Chapter 7: Seeing Light in a Dark Place................................40

Chapter 8: Potential Within...45

Chapter 9: Transitions in Progress..50

Chapter 10: The Forming of Language 54

Chapter 11: A Win with Confidence 59

Chapter 12: Disciplinary Action 65

Chapter 13: The Human Balance Beam..................................69

Chapter 14: Expectation Season...74

Chapter 15: Being Responsible Cost 79

Chapter 16: Believe What You Are Dreaming 82

Chapter 17: Start to Finish..85

CONTENTS

PREFACE

Nothing in life comes easy as a growing person. I've witnessed poverty, struggle, losses, mental breakdowns, and so much more. Things that make it seem all impossible to come back from or to come out of. A deceived mind is a terrible thing. It is worse when people overlook the truth of themselves and others. I believe in change, which is something that will happen whether we want it to or not. We must always be aware of how and where we are directing it.

The moment you as a person change your mindset about where you are or what you are going through, you start to get a better feeling about life. The key to it all is to live in your corrections, not your faults. We all have made huge, bad decisions at some point, but what if you turn that mistake into an answer to a problem? We all as humans have been in a position where we have not been at our best due to the things we have been through. For most dark moments in life, there is some sunlight coming to help us through it.

The truth of the matter is, we must stop living in what happened to us. It is not easy to move on, but you are hindering yourself from peace, joy, happiness, and a life of fulfillment from within. Being free of misery helps the journey of life sail smoother. You got what it takes except nothing less than who you feel you can be. Remember, God gave us important elements that we must always be mindful of. The power to will, meaning we can get things we think about through actions performed toward them.

So we must be mindful that time is a precious element that must not be abused. It is okay to enjoy your hobbies, but at some point, you must be working on what you have within. Where you really want to go in life. The things you feel that are important to you for personal growth. If you don't feel nothing on the inside, find a way to give your life some type of meaning, something to wake for more than a job.

ACKNOWLEDGMENTS

We go through a tsunami of feelings and situations on the road of life trying to express who we are. In those storms, we lose sight of who we are and destined to be. Life challenges get as tough as a five hundred-piece puzzle. The willpower of GOD is real.

To my mother Debra, the sweetest, nicest, most loving, caring, down-to-earth person I know, thank you for being an unmovable rock in every moment of my life. You always believed in my brothers and me. Those hold-your-head-up and who-your-mother conversations worked. Every mother should always reinstall the fight in a child's weak moments—through the challenges of life, without a person who has been through certain struggles you face, to help bring you through to make it all seem possible to recover from the condition or being broken by our mistakes, the laughing, the failure, and so much more.

To my aunt Latisha, thank you for coaching, mentoring, and being the big sister I always wanted. Not even jail bars could stop you from pushing me in GOD's direction. This has been more than what I could have ever dreamed of. This is proof that we all have well within us to be displayed to the world.

I, being an older brother, have always held myself to greater responsibility so to my brothers Damion, Jermarkus, and my baby brother Darren (RIH). You are all great brothers of mine, and we come from seeds of greatness.

I've grown enough to acknowledge how GOD uses people to set the stage for his purpose without them knowing so. So I will say it's just the gut feeling that we are doing the right thing.

To Christopher, my friend, my dad, if you would never have moved my mother to Memphis after that incident, it is a 99.99 percent chance I would've never gotten to this point. Sometimes we must follow our instinct even when we do not know how it will end up.

INTRODUCTION

....

The *Reintroduction* is to bring light back to self-improvement in life. The message is to help lift one's mind, body, soul, and spirit. We often go through life feeling lost, with no sense of direction and no one to turn to for answers. Many of us want to unleash something so great within us because of what we have been practicing the last few years of our lives, but we're not allowing the great ideas that our great brain or great body operate to its maximum capacity. The reason is because before we knew we had control over our future, we were already broken, stepped on, and crushed by life itself as a child.

As a *Reintroduction*, I'm here to offer and help as a positive guide. To get our minds back to thinking, back to fighting, back to handling day-to-day life challenges. Yes, I, too, have been beaten, broken to pieces, laughed at, and life pulled me apart like a puzzle. One thing I can say is I'm thankful to have my right mind, health, strength, breath in my body to speak, able to walk and give someone what's in me. The *Reintroduction* is introduced to help find that champion, that winner to bring out the best you.

To help you understand, GOD has not left you. He is waiting for you. Many of us, including myself, have asked the question, "If GOD wants me to do something, why he won't just do it himself?" Well, I'm here as a witness to say on the behalf of GOD, when you want some new clothes or shoes, they don't just come to you. You must go get them. When someone needs you, they come get you, and you assist until the job or calling is done. So you have to pray, meditate, and talk to GOD every day to develop your peace of mind for yourself. Do like that addict that can't go without a hit. Give all the energy you have to it.

It must form or become what you expect. You cannot let nothing, I mean nothing—no one, no job, car, a thought, kid, adult, and music—separate you from making your dream happen. You will face many obstacles and challenges will get harder, but the truth is, no human possibly knows what you truly want. How you genuinely want it. How it's supposed to look when it's done. No one but you and your God. So it's time to stop the *don't-nobody-care-about-me* thinking. Don't-nobody-believe-in-me feelings. When the truth is, do you care about you? Do you even believe in you? No person is heavenly obligated to make sure you get out of you what you know is great and feel good to you.

The more consistent you are with being your true self, the more fights you must put in until the person you hate being is gone. Time has come to grow. So here within this material that is presented to you, you shall no longer be regular, hang out with regular people, or feel like you're eating regular food (even if it is the same as what others eat). What I mean is, when you cook yours, believe you cook it the best way to the best perfection prepared by the greatest hands. Season with the best seasonings, cooked at a secret temperature only you know about. So when you put your mouth, you say, "This is it. The greatest taste among others."

You also must be creative with all the work you put out. When you start moving toward the things you feel are true to you, GOD starts to move within you. He is ready to assist you with the greatest life prepared by the greatest hands. The *Reintroduction* is prepared to pull you out, so before I close this, I will say, "It is okay to be you."

CHAPTER 1

....

Acknowledge You Can Do Better

Over a period, we often fall short in everyday life challenges. We wake up to deal with life daily to take care of bills, family, wants, and other needs. Many people go hard to make ends meet, but do they go hard enough to get over the hump far enough to make things easier? Growing up, we watched athletes, artists, actors, and a wide range of entertainers. We see they live the life living their dream. They live what they work hard for. We, indeed, have something in common.

Two things are working hard and paying bills. Yes, they are normal people like you and me. We also have a huge difference within us that set us apart. One class of people work to fulfill their dreams while paying bills and the others work just to pay bills. This should raise a question. Why? I've found two reasons. Reason number one is many of our lives are filled with so much stuff to do. I get it. We get worn out, exhausted, and tired just on the basic requirement of life. We want to give up.

Maybe you had a vision, dream, or something before you grew up as a kid. Some responsibilities down the line of life's blows, you lost sight of it. It is still there in you. The one thing you believe will still work, but you're too afraid to try. You think it is too late; it might not work, you see someone else doing it, or you're too old.

When the truth is you're right on time to pick it up again. Enough life has passed you by that you should at least be ready to put one foot to start. Look at it like this. Burger King sells burgers, fries, and breakfast. Months later came McDonald's; they sell burgers, fries, and breakfast. What made McDonald's still go with that idea even though they saw Burger King selling burgers, fries, and breakfast? That gave McDonald's a reason to open and sell.

Furthermore, they created their own taste and alive came McDonald's. You create your own way of doing stuff. Stop letting stuff that look like it's doing better than how you thought it out put you down. Use it to pump you up. Start telling yourself, "They don't know, but I got the flavor, I got the juice, and I got what it takes."

Reason number two is we have developed an internal disease virus, one that is almost worse than COVID-19. This one doesn't kill you dead as fast, but this one I'm talking about will let you live a full life. It can change the outcome and results in many situations. No, I'm not talking about AIDS. You can stop sweating now. You don't need a pill. This is one no doctor can fix.

As a matter of fact, it is what GOD uses alongside his word, and it's called belief. Your belief system is one of the greatest tools GOD gave to humans and other life upon the earth. It sits next to your willpower. They date each other. They work together so well that the baby they produce is what you become. Wow, that's big; you can become more than a conqueror. You can start to become an over-comer of life challenges. The day you stop believing is the day the window of opportunity closes to you.

A person who doesn't believe in their self and can do something about it is like a walking airhead. Think about how ants carry something we think is too heavy for it to carry. The ant believes it could carry the object back to the nest, so it did. So what about a dog that jumps over a gate that we thought it would never make it over? It's belief system. Think about someone doing something that was a bit challenging, but they completed it. They believed and saw themselves finishing.

The great thing about belief is it's always accessible to us. Rather, we choose to use the tool or not. So your belief system is the most important part of the process. Let's think about the word *better*. What is better? *Better* is the constant improvement of something. Take that and run with it. When a person takes a car to a paint shop, it usually has scratches, dents, and chipped paint. The painter takes the car and removes the dents. Then it goes into a primer stage where the car is stripped of all its paint. It has no color; it's even more scuffed than when it came in. Then the painter applies a coat of color on the vehicle. The color alone is dull, so the painter applies a coat of gloss to make the paint job to look better. The more coats of gloss the painter applies, the better the paint job looks and the shinier the vehicle becomes.

Even you, too, can add a coat of gloss to your life to look better, feel better, and do better. Let us ask ourselves a couple of questions. How do you feel about where you are in life? How do you feel about the accomplishments you have made? Have you made any that will contribute to where you are truly wanting to go in life? Can you go farther? Do you have what it takes to go harder and go far? Every day I woke up, I looked in the mirror and didn't like what I saw as a person, who I was becoming. So what I did was start saying to myself, "I can do better. I'm going to do better no matter the cost. I will be who I desire to be at all costs."

Yes, life was winning, but to have a thought of *I can do better* was all I needed to get started in the fight of life. I have been fighting life back with every muscle, every thought, every piece of love, and every piece of pain. No more just sitting around to let it beat me with its beatable challenges. Me seeing others give up had drawn me to do the same because it seemed to be the easier thing to do. Not knowing it was creating a lazy mind, a lazy person, a procrastinator, a dream killer, and a giver upper. I started to feel like this must be it, I'm tired, which was me thinking and operating in my low thinking of thoughts.

I was also a loser at the game of life. I heard something within me laughing at my failures until I got fed up and tired and decided, "No more, I'm about to change this. I want to be greater than I've been before." So I ask myself, "How do I get better? How do I get bigger? How do I get greater? How do I start?" Well, the first thing I did was start to search within myself and pray.

CHAPTER 2

....

Prayer Will Bring You Out

Growing up as a child in Greenville, Mississippi, my grandmother, Mrs. Jones (RIH), used to take us to church. We hated it because we did not understand it. Before services started, the pastor prayed. First, we saw all the adults standing with their heads bowed as the pastor prayed. As we got older and moved to Memphis, Tennessee where my mother was introduced to Islam, we were taught how to pray like the Muslims. My mother prayed on her rug, and my brothers and I prayed on dried off towels.

Still at that point, I never knew what prayer was, what do you do or what we were praying about nor what we were praying for. As I got older, I always would hear and tell people just to pray about it, not knowing that prayer actually has power. I wish I would have known the power of prayer many years ago or an understanding to some degree. I didn't always pray. I was out in field headfirst like many of you. I didn't understand there was something that my mother and grandmother was planting in me. A secret that is available to everyone. Before I knew what prayer offered, my life was hard. Many of my decisions didn't work in my favor. I quit and got fired from permanent jobs where I could have moved up in the company to support my family. I lived a very loose life that was reckless and unnecessary. Just like you, I was doing stuff I had no business doing. If I understood and was using my prayer power or maybe had some understanding what pray is, what it produces, and how it helps, I believe I would have been farther along in life, but I guess looking at where I am now, it played out kind of how it was supposed to.

Every company I've worked for has meetings. These meetings tell us how the company is doing, where the company is going, and how the company is doing on a day-to-day basis to get there. What needs to happen to improve? Also, companies have quarters which are four phases a year. Each phase, they check to see how the production of the company is doing according to the company's plan. If things are doing well, they have picnics and things of sort for everyone. If it's doing bad, they find the reason why and fix the problem. Rather, they have to let some people go or hire more people for help.

You could have a big company with God, but the only way is through prayer. God should be on your board of decision makers for the company. It takes time to form a real relationship with God. Are you willing to wait it out? Prayer is the type of power that helps you get things you want and most importantly things that are yours. It's okay to pray about stuff, but make it easy on yourself by simply asking for what's yours. It's okay to ask for your identity, your gifts, and talents which are things that are yours. I know how it is when you don't have these important pieces to your life puzzle.

It's better when you can use your creativity in a way that makes you feel important or serve your purpose to the world. Many times, we get so wrapped up in life we don't even think about praying. Prayer is the phone to heaven that helps you get answers. Many times, when we pray, stuff seems like it takes forever to come. The truth is a lot of the stuff we pray for is not ours. People often pray for money bags and bags of money. God sends an idea. We say, "No, I didn't ask for work. I asked for money."

The truth for the money you asked to receive takes work. So that's why God sent an idea, so you prepare yourself for the money you are asking for. The reason why is because we have been misusing everything we have already. So until we learn to appreciate and use what we have properly, God keeps you locked out. Once you start the process of the idea, go back and talk to your board of the company.

Once you talk like you got it figured out, get ready; a well-worked out plan is on the way. While you were planning, God already had it figured out. It usually starts with him letting you know he wants you to do something for him. We have two kinds of prayer we can do. One is a silent prayer. You know, the one when you're in the back of the police car on the way to jail. The one where you're on your last strike on your job, and you come in late. This type of prayer is good for quick moments, but for them to really work in your favor, you have to be connected. The second is a verbal prayer. This is the one where you develop the real strength you need. This is the one to help overcome the fear of life. It's basically you communicating to get the authority you need to operate your gift.

This type of prayer helps to solve problems that are bigger than you. When the answers come, you have to be available to hear. Most of the time, we get the answer from these prayers, but because of the noisy life we live, we either look over it or miss it when it comes. Let's think about when we go to church. In the beginning, we all have to stand. The pastor prays for us as a whole group. He delivered what God gave him in his heart to say. How or where does the pastor get his power in order to speak powerful words to awaken the senses? For the pastor to do what he or she does, they have to have some alone time with the board of their company, God.

How does the pastor get the building able to pay staff off and more? It's through the private relationship. You don't see him or her when they are in prayer alone, working the contract with God. Asking God for the money. You wonder how you have people that are joyful and happy all the time. It's because they have been in private asking for joy, asking for happiness, and asking for peace. The private relationship must be developed to live an abundant life.

Once I started praying and paying tithe, my life changed. My life started to change along with hearing and doing positive things. If you want prayer to work for you, apply these three steps:

1. *Believe in the unseen.* Before there were cars, there were horses. Someone prayed, and God gave them an idea. The idea was unseen and unheard of. They didn't start out with

all the stuff they needed in order to bring the car idea to life. They stuck with it until it became what they saw. When you really believe in something, you put all hope and your attention into it. Nothing gets in the way. Remember, you are creative enough to make it anyway. Keep picking up the phone to your board of decision makers and work it out. Don't give up; give all in.

2. *Act on the unseen.* After you talk to the board and get it worked out, understand that only you know what it's supposed to look like, feel like, taste like, or sound like. Depend on no one to get it done the way you want it. Do it and when you do it, do it with the mindset and pride that people are going to love what you are offering. Make sure your action is from the heart.

3. *Become the unseen.* When you are on the job, you become what they hired you for. Think about warehouse workers. Pickers pick, packers pack, and forklift operators operate the forklift. Basically, you become what you signed up for. So the stuff you pray about look forward to becoming that. Speak the way it's supposed to sound, dress the way it's supposed to look. Become it enough so you speak it and represent it how you talked about it to God.

There's nothing wrong with change. Every second, our movement and thought change, and these changes don't affect us until the direction is acted upon. Be the example you want to see. Once you become what is unseen, expect things to be different because everything about you will be.

You know prayer is something you can truly and honestly freestyle. I say that because just about every day you will pray about something different. I started out with a simple prayer: "God, I'm tired of this life. I need help. Show me what to do and how to do it. Amen." Then I started to do small things to help my situation. No, I didn't pray every day starting off. I felt like things were changing for me with the action I was putting in with the prayer.

EMANUEL JONES

I had to identify who I was and what I genuinely wanted to do or become. So my prayer went from what it was to "God, I need help to identify who I am. What's my identity, what am I here to do? What is my mission, what is my gift? Help me identify my purpose, amen." I kept doing what I was doing and working a little harder to change what was at hand. My financial situation was bad. Bills coming left and right. Me constantly creating that.

One day, God came to me and gave me exactly what I asked for. My gift, my identity, and my purpose. I became very afraid and said this is not for me. This is not who I am. I didn't see it. I didn't see me doing that which he brought to me. I ran from it for ten plus years, but it didn't leave me alone. It stuck with me through thick and thin, the good and the bad. Years passed, and I still didn't act on what was there until the death of Miss Jones, my grandmother, and going through a gun charge at the same time. I felt I lost myself in a way, but in a way, I could control it. On the brink of that, I knew myself, meaning I knew what I will and won't do. It seemed that my life was coming to an end.

To keep from feeling that way, I kept myself busy not to think about what I was going through. I was working a job, working on cars, hauling junk, moving people, etc. Whatever it took not to think about my situation. Not to think about my own failure. Until God came and asked me to assist him with something. I was being exposed to something greater than me, but I felt, "What have got I to lose?"

So my prayer now again elevated to:

> God, let your will work in me. Give me the power, wisdom, knowledge, understanding, courage, charisma, and character from the greatest place.
>
> Thank you for my health, strength, and being in my right mind. Help me to do what's needed for this mission. Don't go soft on me, Lord, because what you are calling me to do is not an easy task. Bring the right people in my life, remove the people who are not for me. Let me know when I meet the right people who are

20

for what we are seeking to accomplish. Guide me along the way. Protect me from anyone or anything that's against us. God, protect my family with the best angels. Lord, protect my friends with the best angels. Come into their lives to help them conquer themselves and accomplish their mission. Help those who are appointing me in the right direction. I like to put all these things in your hands. In Jesus's name, amen.

So from that point, my life has been changing and I knew it, so I had to change my thinking.

CHAPTER 3

....

Thinking Greatness

When thinking about greatness, you have to also think about the word *respect*. I say this because anything great has a certain level of respect. All the great people I know are well-respected. Just think of how impactful great people really are. Greatness requires respect, respect requires discipline, and discipline requires respect for who you want to be. You will always have someone to disagree with you. Maybe not all people.

Let's take the word *think* and break it down a bit. The word *think* are ideas or thoughts that are conceived in one's mind about something we don't see. So when you use your brain before you start a task, you think about how to do it first. As you are performing the duty of the task, you think of how to finish the task. When you think while on the task and form thoughts, you are also gathering new information.

New information means now your thoughts can add a new updated information and throw out the old. Let's take our cell phones for example. Some of us buy phones every time one comes out. So you may not know what an update is. If you are like me, you can hold onto your phone as long as you can. As long as it rings, you can answer it, receive texts, and get on the Internet. You know after time goes by, many new phones have come out. Our phones give us an option to update the current system of the version of the phone we use. Moreover, the apps we have on the phone update as well to get the better and latest version of the app. Notice you don't take the phone to a store to do it or anyplace; it is done right there with you where you are. Hold up; you have to push the button to activate it. What does it take to activate you? What buttons do you have to push in order for you to start an update on your life? How many times can I say just do something new with yourself?

It's possible to get out more and want to do new things. Whatever it is could possibly grow you. When talking about just the thought of greatness, what does that really consist of? Just the thought of greatness is huge let alone to become it. Some of the things that qualified people as great is dedication, self-motivation, consistency, willingness, and many more attributes. The number one thing that any person must master is the character of whom they ought to become—your character's biggest role. Becoming great, your character has so much influential power that it determines what level of greatness you fall under.

It determines how serious people will take you based upon the way you carry yourself. Your character is either your door opener or your door closer. It can take you to the next level or can take you out. Your character must be developed and designed for growing purposes only. So you must be sure what you are fighting for is what you really want. No one starts out great. Greatness always starts small and must be groomed along the way. There is a great amount of pressure to become great. Your greatest movie stars, basketball players, football stars, and many more all had to go through grooming before the big screen. They all had to go through mess ups, failures, feeling they didn't have enough to get the job done, and someone telling them they don't have what it takes. Think about what made those people not give up and keep going.

They all developed a mindset and a heart that said, "I'm the greatest at what I do." They all took the pressure and frustration and became strong where they were weak in some areas. We all know the story about wine—the longer it sits, the better it gets. Wine is made from grapes on a vine. Yes, grapes are one of my favorites but to make my point, the grapes that are sitting on the vine will rot, but the grapes that are smashed to make wine is in the process of becoming better grapes but in a new formation. So you can be the grapes on a vine and wait to see if someone will purchase you before you rot, or you can choose to become remade to be used for the greater purpose. You can be on the vine like others, or you can show what you got to offer. To become anything on a good level, a higher level than mediocracy will require a great amount of energy. You have to have the type of energetic attitude that can withstand going against your normal.

What do people say about you to you? How to get up when you fall. How to be strong when you are weak and much more. When thinking about greatness, open your mind to all possibilities, but don't let it frighten you. Just be prepared. The only way you will make it to greatness is learning what's needed and being able to constantly move past obstacles that will come unexpectedly. You'll get this; I believe in you. It's not easy to think positive in most negative situations. So when they start to come, I find something positive in every negative situation no matter what.

Yes, life will hit you with cruel curveballs and some boulders. When this happens, it's about how you come back off a lick like that. How you get back up determines where you stand and how you stand. Some stuff can come and try to wipe you out. When these moments happen, I simply keep going. If it's something I couldn't handle at the time, I put it on the back burner so I can handle the next thing at the moment. You have to have a strong mind going through life. Family will chew you up and spit you out with ease. So how do we protect that here? How do we protect our mind? I must ask, "What do you think about when you wake up in the morning? What's your first thoughts? What do you do to keep yourself strong? What do you listen to?"

I already know that when it's time to get up, you wake up in the mind frame of "I got to get up and go deal with these people at work." You wake up tired with a slight headache, feeling sluggish. I was there, too, and some days I still feel all that pain and pressure. How do you change that? What I did was I simply started using affirmations: "I'm great, I'm going to have a great day. I'm the best at what I do. I am who they need, this is not where my life will end. Today, I will do better than yesterday."

You get the picture. You have to get in your mind you are the best at what you do. The way you think can create either a peaceful life or an unpeaceful life. Changing your thinking will take you out of your comfort zone. This is what you use to break the cycle of basic thinking; it is not easy, but you can do it. You have to challenge your mind every day to something new. Whether it's exercising or reading a book, listening to positive music or messages, something out of your normal. Don't be afraid of you helping yourself; you will see in the long run. Another thing is keeping positive thoughts is a must when people call you with negative. Turn it into positive to help them see the positive situation. What kind of people do you hang around? Are they positive people? This is one thing that can affect every last one of your thoughts.

When you are doing things to feed your flesh, how do you feel doing it? I used to drink due to being depressed and all the other things to make me feel bad. I changed my thinking to fight this cruel life back. When I go all day doing things toward my mission, I'm accomplishing goals. I changed my thinking to be better, to be greater, and to become the greatest. Remember, you have to turn it positive at all costs. I know not every situation is meant to be positive, but don't let it put your mind in a box or a place of no return. Protect your head. Remember, negative thoughts dump out your head. Stay away from negative energy. Having a strong mind comes with replacing stuff and creating space.

CHAPTER 4

....

Making Room in a Crowded Place

When you wake up in the morning and come to your right mind, how do you feel? Many of us feel cluttered. We don't have the good feeling like we rested. A lot of times, many of you awaken with headaches and hangovers.

Have you ever looked or felt like your life is just too crowded? Think about it. You got to go to work, got to go get the children, got to go kick it with the friends, got to go see what's on Facebook, got to catch the favorite TV shows, got to find something to eat. All carry a different amount of weight. They all have done one thing and that's take up space in you.

You walk around with it all day every day, carrying extra weight. Imagine putting on a twenty- or thirty-pound workout vest every morning and you not wearing it for working out purposes. It's just there for you to walk around with. This is the extra weight every day according to the things you do. Think about going to the DMV, the grocery store on the first or the third, or maybe walking into the food stamp office—all crowded places. Makes you want to turn around but you can't because you don't have the room to. Imagine this being your brain. Just think about how much stuff we walk around with day in and day out in our mind that is not important to be there.

We have let some stuff live within us longer than it's supposed to. I have a question. When does some of these energy-draining freeloading thoughts expire? Not going to say much here but a lot of the things we carry on the inside can weigh us down instead of pick us up. A truck is made to carry a certain amount of weight. The more the weight limit is exceeded though, the lower the back of the truck gets, thus the slower the truck drives. Also, since you're forcing more weight, then there will be more wear and tear on the engine and transmission. So basically, the truck doesn't last as long as it's supposed to.

You are no different than the truck. Are you someone who has created a normal full of things that don't matter? Things that keep you from reaping the benefits of your full potential. You have to create a new normal for yourself. Start getting rid of the weight. You are born and built with this capacity. Some of us have a larger capacity than others. For example, mine might be a pint-size milk jug and yours might be a gallon-size milk jug. So if either is full, we can't put anything else in it. If we are pouring liquid out, then we will have some space to add more.

Look at who you deserve to be and what you deserve to look like. You are a representative of God. If you are full all the time, how can God put something in something that's always full? A lot of stuff that you're trying to get away from may never leave you alone, but you can leave it. These things come to contain you to one way of living, one way of thinking, and one way of acting. It is upon you to be strong enough mentally to see your normal and not be a part of what was. I stopped drinking and can still be around people that do so. It's was hard for me; yes, I had been drinking twenty years plus.

It was one thing that made me a procrastinator and many more things that were hindering me from my destiny. When I stopped, I gained more access than I've ever had before in my life. For all the stuff you carry, answer me this—what are you gaining from it other than hurt? You only live once. Let it go. Find something positive to listen to when you wake up and before bed. Let's start working on getting rid of some of that stuff. Yes, someone may have wronged you, but haven't you also wronged someone too? Now maybe you're wrong wasn't as bad as theirs.

The way you felt when someone wronged you, think about when you did something wrong to somebody else. You make them feel how you feel right now—hurt. You have to approach life with a new strategy to heal yourself. You start treating life as if you are healing it toward others. You get what you put out, remember.

Now there are some people I know, you have to put them in their place, and that's fine. The big thing here is you're building a *new you,* so don't get bent out of shape. I once heard a person say, "The best ability is availability." This means, when you have a clear mind free from a lot of the horrors, frustrations, and stress, you can get the things done on time, not rushing. That new positive energy you're putting out starts bringing new stuff your way. If you're cluttered, crowded, and unavailable, you keep losing out. These are the reasons why you must free your mind, so you can think fresh new ideas and go act on them. A boxer can't win a fight with stuff piled up in his head. He would not be able to focus on his opponent well enough. A tightrope walker can't walk across the rope with stuff piled up in his head. He will fall because of his own distractions. You get the point. A few things you can do to clear your head:

1. Talk to the person who hurt you. Understand you're not talking to them in the sense that you are looking for an apology; you are talking to them to leave it there to get it off you. You are going for closure whether they agree with you or not. If things start to get heated, keep your cool and simply walk away. You trying is all that matters.
2. Start feeding your mind new stuff. The old stuff will rise; you have the power to keep rejecting it. Keep putting in positive mind food. Over time, you will begin to see and feel the difference.
3. Look, we've always heard "Get around some people that's doing good things in the world." The energy of these types of people is what you want to be around to rub off on you. The energy you see them put in is the same energy that

brought them through to find their niche. After all you've been through it, you owe it to yourself to try to be better.

4. Stop the *I-know-everything* thought because, to be real with you, it's okay not to know certain stuff. This creates room to get more in once you realize all the things you don't know. Stop using your pains, fears, and failures for a crutch. You are what you are trying to get others to feel about you. If you are someone who wants people to feel sorry for your situation, just look how sorry you look and feel on the inside. Be the most joyful person you can be no matter what.

When you are approaching people in that low operation of thinking, people say, "Here comes sorry Joe or Sue." Think about a time when you really had it and your stress level was low. You probably were a person who cared about yourself more. So if you are a person who shows gratitude and certain positive things, people feel good around you. And they love to eat off that type of energy. Living with a clear mind or a mind with room to receive more is a comfortable way to live. Remember, you are what and how you think. Upon making space, realize that you are not just clearing the space for yourself; you are clearing it to be available to where you are heading, which will be helping someone else be a better version of their selves.

This is important to do because here, you create space for opportunity and growth that you want. You know having a crowded mind can be the very reason you feel tired and exhausted. You can't do more with this weight on you, and it actually weighs a whole lot more than you imagine. I know the feeling of having kids, no transportation, bills due and all. No one to help pay, everybody around you broke, or at least say they are. Don't want to set your pride to the side to ask who you know you can go get it from because you ask so many times. I know what it feels like when it seemed like everyone is winning but you, and you feel like you are doing so much.

"I got three jobs, and I'm still broke. What am I doing wrong?" Well, let's focus on removing stuff that's stored within that should be removed. What's living in your mind for free that's not bringing you to your goal or level of peace or what you think you should be in life? It could be a car sitting in your yard there needing to be fixed, but you don't have the funds to do so. Listen to me: "Get rid of it, and take the loss." Once I learned that small simple trick about life, burdens lifted. The weight started to fall off me. My life started to change.

It could be an argument you had with someone. Don't walk around thinking about what some foul things a person may have said. Listen to me: "Don't let it live in your mind." When you know you are greater, it could be a loss of a close one. Listen to me: "Yes, it happens, but leave it where it is. It happened for a reason. You are still here. Keep your mind clear of the happening. That is one of the best investments you can make in life. No one can make you take whatever is taking the space off your mind, only you. It's your brain. No, it's not easy."

So how do you replace negative weight with positive weight? Positive weight is usually lighter than negative weight. Negative weight beats you down, and positive weight builds you up. So put in positive thoughts when you remove things because you don't just want open space to invite the negative back in. You may have something such as a bill, the need to get food, or whatever it is. Don't let it beat you; you beat it by not letting it get to you. You know what is needed to be done to keep the pressure off you. Once you get this going, well, guess what's coming next? More opportunity.

CHAPTER 5

....

Open Opportunity

Time after time, I've spoiled, messed up, missed out, and misused plenty of opportunities. Opportunities are nothing but open chances to open and close doors in life. There are hundreds of different doors of possibility and chances. We are presented every day, all day, a chance to do something more than what we did yesterday. Do we always take advantage of it though? The answer is no!

People hate the thought of starting something new because they have settled where they are. It's okay to settle but don't expect much from it. You have stopped your growth when you decided to stop. Life is about growing. The moment you stop growing, it brings all the things you don't want—stress, depression, and all the other things that bring unwanted pain. Don't get comfortable if you know you get tired of doing the same task every day. That's not fulfilling your soul, spirit, or mind. Basically, what makes you happy?

We are designed to learn new things. We close doors before we know where or what we can really earn from it. I've heard Myles Monroe say retirement is not in the Bible anywhere. Over the years, I've learned sometimes certain opportunities knock to take you to the next level or prepare you for it. People being who they are skip over the unknown to still struggle in the known. Many of us think we are taking big chances when we are only scratching the surface.

Let me ask you this—what stops a panhandler from going to get a job in today's time? Many places are hiring with no background check. Low self-esteem, drugs, alcohol, fear, and failure all will help destroy the mentality of overcoming what could be overcome. I know some of them are truly disabled. I'm not talking about them. So when we think about it and look at many of our conditions, we have become similar to a panhandler because they became dreamless, with no vision, and not creating real chances to better their situation.

The way they are on the corner is the way many of us are at our jobs. Just accepting life for what it is and where you have landed. When you get over the fear of doing things on your own, you open the mind to "how can I make this happen?"

Then you look at all the possibilities, make a choice, and make it happen. When opportunity comes, it comes in one form wrapped like a gift waiting to be conquered. It is untouched potential. Understand all opportunity is packed with more opportunity. So is potential; it's packed with more stuff that can be used. Even when it seems it has run out, look, there's a little more.

How creative can you get with what you have? You will begin to see most ideas you think are to add value to your life. Some ideas tell you to subtract some things. Some say add. If you are smart enough, you will understand how to multiply for the ideas and when to divide. Just think about it. Everyone has thought of something and said "*No*" in our mind about it. Thought to ourselves, *I'm going to be rich one day.* The thing is, we didn't act on the idea, so we never knew how far we could've gone with it.

Many times, we allow our circumstances to make decisions for us. To change that, work against the circumstance and take your chances on your opportunity. Many times, people don't see any further than where they are. So to change this, we must recognize what we have outgrown. Where are we trying to go? What will get us there?

The one thing that should always build thoughts to give you opportunity is the struggle you are constantly in, which we should not let determine our outcome. We see family, friends, and others struggle all the time. Is it because it looks familiar? You've been doing it so long you don't see no other way out because nobody around you got out yet.

Well, here's the news: *you are the way out.* Look at it this way. They are waiting on you to lead them out. Buckle down and take the blows, so you can change, create, and restore the absent opportunity they don't see. GOD will act on what you act on. If you turn on your seriousness, he turns on lights, so you can see what you got. Think about it in the beginning—the earth was dark. GOD said "Let there be light" because of the need to see what he was working with.

Now if you can picture yourself being in a dark earth, all you need is for GOD to say let there be light to you. How do you get this to happen? Simple—prayer and acting on what positive ideas you get. Understand there will be some tests and trials you will face to see if you are serious before the doors are opened wide. So the door will open just enough to peek in, but you can't walk in yet. You can't open it wide enough to walk through until you develop enough strength in an area to push it a little bit. Then it cracks opens a little more. So you need to get stronger on different levels constantly to keep moving the door open.

Once it's open, walk through and enjoy it, but understand there is another door and another door and another door. You must be focused enough to open them. The same way you fought to open the first one. You can use the same tools to open the next one, but the only problem you might run into is the tools you have will get dull. So as you walk, keep shaping your tools. You know that two of the greatest tools humans have are the power to think creative ideas and the ability to work toward them.

Ideas become monuments of life. Look at some of the stuff that will be here on earth after we die. Look how some ideas have exploded into greater pieces of work. Look at how you once before thought about doing something but didn't do it, and it looked like GOD gave it to someone else. You saw them using or doing what you thought about. How did it make you feel? The greatest tool you can ever possess is the power to will. When you operate this tool correctly, you can and will become dangerous to some things and some people.

I've heard Myles Monroe say your willpower is so strong that not even GOD can stop it. Your willpower is the ability to manifest ideas. Many do not know how to use this or really activate it. The simple way to tell you how is to keep moving toward your goals no matter what. Your mind and body is a factory that produces ideas to try. It's upon you to bring what you see and feel from the unseen place within you to reality for us to see here on earth. You want to fulfill or find your purpose? Act on the opportunity within you first before acting on opportunities outside of you.

You know opportunity can be good or bad. Now you have fresh new thoughts, you feel good about who you are and what you are becoming. Opportunity is something you create for yourself. Don't wait on no one to give it to you. Learn how to use what you have until you get to the place where you are going. A person who sells drugs starts small and moves up when they gain enough money to buy more supply. A car salesman might start with one car sale. Use the money and buy two. Use that money and buy four. A person with a nine-to-five might not have the best checks but should be putting something to the side if they really have a dream. Once you get enough to start your small thing, use your workplace to get a little clientele, but be careful because most workplaces don't allow people to sell outside products. Find a way to grow what you want to be involved in. If you're sitting and waiting your turn, get your ass out of the line. Move yourself to the front of the line by creating your own different opportunity.

So you can struggle not getting a lot from your job or you can struggle building something that will pay twice, maybe three times more than your job. Embrace life, your hustle, your job, the things you love and care about, and they will embrace you back. The greatest way to keep opportunity or constantly making it greater is the person you are and also the person you are running to become.

CHAPTER 6

....

Bridge the Gap

The whole concept of this project is to help come back to, fix, and patch some broken pieces within you. We all have been broken, torn apart, and ripped to pieces by family, friends, and strangers. We are people with emotions that trigger actions. Emotions are sometimes good and sometimes bad. They are like built-in sensors that trip when we feel violated. Once tripped in violation mode, it's hard to call off the anger that comes with it. We've all done sporadic things to trip someone's emotional alarm off on purpose before. There are many of us who had no intention to, but it happened.

Emotions are also what gets us in some deep trouble. Men and women are emotional, and sometimes I wonder who is the most emotional. To me, women should be more because she was built to nurture more. The man is supposed to be able to handle the pressure a little more. We have entered a peculiar time where it seems the man has been just as emotional. Why? Growing up in my time, men had a code, for example, and a strategy of what to do. Now the strength of the man's mentality is being challenged in a way that he is allowing the pressure of the test to beat him up internally.

Not all men are facing the same challenges today, but if you are, there is a great chance that you are being broken by GOD for preparation. What I mean by this is that you are being shaped to be used for better purposes. Many reject or go against this calling of transformation, only to end up still in the same place in life. The fight we all are fighting is to bring the man back to himself. We are and have fallen into a trick bag that doesn't allow the man to grow or explore his worth, his true work, and most importantly himself.

I, too, was a part of this system. I didn't recognize that I wasn't growing mentally. It kept me limited to what I could do. I've always been a writer, but because of my comfort zone and fear of walking away from my familiarity into something unfamiliar seemed impossible, I procrastinated. I hate to say this, but some men are still boys mentally. Afraid to grow up. Wanting someone to carry us. This is the most crippling thing that could happen to any of us. Instead of leaning toward doing things on our own, many would rather do a little to say they are trying, just to keep the help from someone else. Basically, they are leaning toward needing someone rather than making way for themselves. I, again, have been guilty of this system. Let's do a self-test. How much have you evolved since high school? I'm saying this for you to be honest with yourself. Are you living in your *faults*, or are you living in your *corrections*? This makes a big difference when you are living in your faults; you are in the worst place of life.

You have created a comfort for it to bother you. When you are living in your own corrections, you can actually breathe better and think clearer. When you create this type of space, you are making yourself able to live with blows and how to overcome them. Understand it's all a creation. Not saying you created it all but you can create the atmosphere you want. Many of us treat our life like bad car owners. One problem happens, and we don't fix it. Another problem happens, then we say, "I'll fix it later," but later never comes until the car is on its last leg. It would run a lot longer if problems are handled when they come about. They look crazy at the car like it's supposed to fix itself.

We have more excuses as to why we didn't make it than the reasons why we did. So many people have fallen out over stuff so small that it makes no sense. Families are not close anymore; friendships have been broken up over some stuff that they should have been bigger than. Funny thing is, people are always looking for a way to get over on each other.

This is one of the major problems we face among each other today. The system of loyalty is broken. So much manipulation is going on it makes no sense. I don't blame people because the world we live in is built on it. So we have been secretly taught the skill without knowing we were being programmed to do so. We have been getting manipulated our whole life. So it's in us; it's a form of trickery. It's a get-over method. Many people, not all, start their thinking with *How can I get over*? It has broken up so many relationships, family, friends, and business partners.

Manipulation is not a bad thing when it's used toward the correct system, not to violate people. I learned over the years that without GOD, many things can happen, but the question is, "Am I doing the right thing?"

Many people create problems for themselves because they don't take the time to think the whole situation out before acting on it. We go headfirst. That's the wrong way of doing it. We are people who deal with people and should be figuring ways to keep the system going for each other. Ever wonder what's your purpose on earth? It's to solve a problem that you understand on your level while you are growing and to keep the system of self-improvement going to impact those around you. There's more to that, but this is just to give you a little on what I've learned.

Whether it's babysitting or helping a stranger with gas for their vehicle, you must do something from your heart at some point. The more we do things from our heart, the more we have a chance to promote and rebuild the lost substance of our community. I understand there are people you feel should apologize to you before you talk to them again. Understand you have and are creating the same magnet affect. I'm willing to bet the same way you are treating someone badly; someone is treating you the same way somewhere else in your life right now. This way of doing things doesn't allow life to line things up the way you thought them out. It keeps you off balance, out of alignment, because the alignment of GOD is to treat people how you want to be treated.

Many say they have bad luck, and that's not it. They have gotten out of alignment trying to be what they are not. GOD has given all humans one of his greatest powers, and it's forgiveness. When you learn how to apply it, it's a relief, a burden off you. Just as I talked about in chapter 4, "Making Room in a Crowded Place," the more you free your mind from problems, the more peace you bring to your life. No, not all people will agree with you on certain things, but a peace of mind is what you want. I know you've heard don't let stuff live in your mind for free before. So don't neglect the people you can go to and make it right. Do it for your peace of mind.

Many times GOD tells us to call, pull up, and talk to people that we know are not going to be on the same page. Check your approach sometimes. I know the feeling, but after those conversations, you get a relief and a peace of mind. If you have someone you need to apologize to, stop being petty—do it. None of us have forever on the earth, but what if in the afterlife, you carried everything you have now? Think about that. Some of us are so beat and hurt so badly on the inside that if it was true, your afterlife would be just as painful as your life is now. Every day we wake should be a day toward correction or bettering.

I've been down that hurt rode, and I always thought, *What if in the next life, I had to use what I got to make it through it?* Also I've thought, *What if what I've become in this life, I have to be in the next?* Looking at me and my situation at the time, no, I am not living this over again. So I figured how to grow, which is an important part of life. There's not a person I know who doesn't need someone to stand up for them at some point in their life.

I have not always found or turned to GOD in many of my situations. Let me tell you when I did, I got answers and let him lead me. What if in the afterlife you were to receive ten times back what you gave in life? What will you be getting back? I can see some of you now need to be more positive in your thinking, the way you treat others, and anything you tie yourself to. When talking about building bridges with people, know what you are doing. You are making an agreement to hold your end of the bargain. Must I say everyone doesn't hold their end of the bargain always? It starts out that way, but remember, everyone has their own vision, their own way of how they want things to be for themselves.

So with that being said, always go in knowing that this could end at any moment. When it starts to happen and people don't want to go farther with you, be prepared. To build healthy relationships, apply certain principles such as consideration, accountability, discipline, same-page operation just to name a few. You have to make sure you are all or nothing on your end. So if things go sour, it doesn't fall on you internally. You can't allow someone else wrong drag you down; they'll get what's coming to them. You must find a way to complete the journey.

Yes, it will hurt like other things you've been through, but that's GOD's way of shaping you so the next person, level, or stage you deal with, you will recognize the default long before it happens again. You started something for it to grow, and it's your responsibility to make sure you birth it how you see it. Remember, you are the greatest at what you do on your level. Being mindful of the bridges, we build everybody not for everybody.

If you operate on level 10 and someone operates on a 2, it's not going work. If the 2 can't at least come to a 7 to be somewhat close to the 10, it will not work. Everyone has different agendas. Some will stick around to help, and some people will go the other direction. They will leave because one, it's not going in the same direction or two, it's not moving at their speed. Always stay in the lane of what works for you.

CHAPTER 7

....

Seeing Light in a Dark Place

Imagine you being an ink pen in life. What would your pen be writing to the world? What kind of ink would you leave on people to remember you? How much would you write to get your point across? Some pens have stopped moving because your life has hit writer's block. Writer's block is when someone's life has become dry. They do stuff over and over trying to fill the dryness with stuff that won't work. It's like working in a warehouse as a line worker. You come to the same machines every day. You have the same conversations every day. The same people come to work with the same problems and lies. The chance of growth there is slim. You feel boxed in. Do you see how unfulfilling that sounds?

That's how many lives are in and outside a warehouse. Not producing any true excitement anymore. Funny how stuck up and divided people are, suffering more than they are gaining from it. A lot of our lives are like animals that wander off from the flock. They get lost and have to adapt to an environment and that puts them under more pressure. That animal ends up in many risky positions. Let's talk about the environment of something. A plant grows in a plant environment. It doesn't start the process until you place it under dirt. After being placed under dirt, it sprouts up. It becomes a flower, bush, fruit, tree, and vegetable. If the seed is taken away from what was growing it, it will shock and kill the seed or plant.

People, on the other hand, are born in families with people who have traveled many roads. So our environment is pretested before we are born to help make it easy for us to know what will help and what will not. It's pretested to help you with which direction you are to go in life. What is a bad environment for a human? A bad environment for a person is where they are not growing as an individual. You can't climb a mountain without mountain-climbing gear.

Many want success, riches, and all that come with it that looks like a good life, but are they putting themselves in position to become? The step to make it can't be skipped over. Are you creating and equipping yourself with the correct gear to get there? Are you going through the process of low-paying jobs and creating a way out of what seemed to be no way? Are you giving time to grow mentally in areas you want to go? Set a pace for yourself; develop daily goals to hit a target. This will help get to the major goal over time. It all just takes a little at a time.

I know what you want is big and there's not enough money and you don't have the help. You feel you are not smart enough, and you're waiting for the right time when everything is lined up just right. Know it will never be right until you make it right. It all has to be created. This is the greatest part of you and the journey where your creativity becomes outspoken. Look at it this way—the length of life is the pace you set for where you are heading. Meaning you can be in the race of life but it goes to the one who endures to the end. You will always be tested before you get to the next level.

School and business proves that. Have you really thought about what it's really going to take to make it or the cost of time and effort? Are you willing to apply the methods that you believe will work? I can remember once I didn't know what road I was traveling; I was just out there moving. I had no vision, no foresight, not even a thought of where I was going. I could not see me starting a business or doing my own thing at all. That to me is darkness and being blind. Life didn't wait on me to get it right either. I had to walk by faith, pray, and develop an ear to hear God in the moments I was unsure until I had seen some light.

There were moments growing up I just knew I was trying my hardest, but was I really? Now looking back, I'm sure I wasn't. I was far away from what I could become. I've always felt it on the inside; with no one to guide me to what I saw and felt, it left me no choice but to pray to the Creator. Once I did so, I started helping people. The thing that was inside of me started to get fulfilled. I started giving when I know I didn't have it to give; I followed my heart. I gave my last many times but never told anyone; I just kept moving.

All that I went through—from the disappointments, to the failures, to the unfulfilling moments—now all added up. It makes more sense now than it did at the time. All those things and stuff were dirt for me to come up through, like a planted seed in the ground that's ready for harvest. Only through prayer and conversations with God I learned what and how to use my dirt, my hurt, my mess ups, my failures, my disappointments, my tears, my internal pain. The way you do it is to live in your corrections, not all of what you've been through. Build a space to correct yourself and live there. Be the best answer for someone else.

The past hurt, but you can do something about it. When you correct your wrongs, you start to promote a peace of mind. Go back to your family members and ask them who they are internally that they never brought out for the world to see. Also, listen to all the trapped potential—things that could've either made that person great, rich, or further in life than they are now. Gather that information and apply it to your journey because you can become someone's dream. Do you know how much of a life-changing legacy you can be for yourself and the future of your family?

Look at who all qualify to change the legacy but didn't. You can be the first; go on with your bad self. Think about how big that is. You giving the children behind you and others around you something more to strive for. *Better is always just one extra step toward where you are going, but great is actually getting there.* Yes, it's hard. Les Brown says, "Well, do it hard."

In order for you to be great at this, it takes a great amount of courage, consistency, motivation, life-changing mindset, and patience. You are traveling a road alone from now on. So don't expect anyone to understand your driven passion. Many will look over and past what you are doing, and few will truly admire you for your works. Remember, you were born not to follow but to lead.

Leaders make sure things get done. So things can and will change for better and greater purposes. So now, leader, what are you going to do? Are you going to continue to follow the same path that's been walked by many, or are you going to stand to walk the path of the few? Always choose the path of the few, and create the path for what's behind you.

Close your eyes and relax your mind. I want you to visualize yourself in the building with customers coming to buy your product. Look at the smiles you put on the faces of people who came to shop with you. In life, we often lost sight of what we once wanted. If you can envision yourself where you want to be every day, no matter what, one day you will get there with the work you put in toward it. You have to believe and have faith in your vision; no one knows it better than you.

So how do you pull this vision to reality? It's hard but simple. The hard part is keeping focus and keeping the vision alive, which is a lot of work from you internally that has to be used externally. Yes, your vision/dream idea can go away. If it goes away, sometimes you get it back. The best thing to do is act on what you have now. The only way you can get stuff out is to proceed with the little you can control. Think of it as a magnet; you have to pull your ideas out of your head into reality. This is very tough, but you can do it. Get a plan together and start. When you start the process, it will seem you are running out of time, but you are not.

When that happens, you need to take a small break and go back at it. The problem is, you have an idea and not enough money and people to help build in the beginning. Accomplish the unaccomplished one step at a time. You will get overwhelmed but take the rest break, get some fresh air, take a few days off, and come to it. Stop looking at the big picture so much and pay attention to the small achievements you have made. Think about some of your big companies; they started small with a guy or lady with an idea. They had to go to work jobs that were unsatisfying to them to get to where they are. You have to treat this as your ticket out. No one else has your ticket—you do. So sometimes you have to put fun and other activities on hold to make sure you cash your ticket in. Until you do, you will never know how much it's worth. Get like Nike and just do it.

CHAPTER 8

....

Potential Within

The world has built walls that are meant to be laws and limitations. We were born with breakthrough power of life's complications. There are levels to you:

1. *Mental level:* This is the level you should get your head strong to fight battles on your journey. Your brain is one of the strongest muscles you have. Lose it, and you lose it all. Once you are mentally fit enough for where you are heading, start going in the direction of your destiny. You don't have to be the smartest person to start. You will meet people with five, ten, fifteen, twenty, or thirty years of experience who will help you get mentally fit more.

    So don't get discouraged because of what you don't see physically by sight. Don't let it bother you that people might not accept you because of what you don't know. They all have been where you are, but how serious will you take it is all that matters. Remember, no one starts on top. Rich or poor, all knowledge has to be taught. The more you keep heading in the right direction, the more *stuff you'll pick up to work with.*

2. *Physical level:* This is the level where you act on your stuff. You also have to be physically fit for this journey. You want

to make sure you can make it. Look at it this way—are you healthy enough to make it to your destiny? When you get there, will you look and feel worn out, tired, or will you look like you are ready for more?

3. *Spiritual level:* This is where you help to push through and fight to win. You find your confidence here. You pay close attention to your spirit and your heart; they will guide you. This is something you must practice developing to know when. Many times, you will not feel it in your spirit, but you must know how to choose rather than to keep going or stop.

There are also levels to how successful you are to become. You will figure this part out once things get rolling. The most important thing you have to remember is don't quit and don't get stuck too long. Every time I quit something, it felt like I was starting over on the same task over and over. That is so tiring, boring, and exhausting. So you must find something that motivates you to keep going no matter what.

Don't allow nothing to stop you from growing. Build what you see and feel. Life is about growing. Look around you, if you are not growing, you might be miserable, stressed, and the rest of the words that make you feel down or bad. Being stuck happens at times. Stuck trying to figure out what the next move is. Meaning you're still working toward your goal. Don't ever be so stubborn and not ask for help because you can be stuck too long and lose momentum.

That will make you want to give up because you become tired and exhausted. Don't hang your life in a closet and shut the door. You have come too far to blow it. Look back at the people who have started something but never made it. They gave up. They let the challenges of life win. If you've taken one step toward your destination, fight to the end of your last breath. Nothing should stop you because nothing stopped you from starting.

So many of us have been on the same level so long that we have made it okay to be there, and it's not. You are failing at the game of life if you have let this set in. The way you break this is first, break the mentality that it's all you will be. GOD made man in his image. Think of it this way—we as humans are born to imitate something or someone. So, therefore, if you are not imitating something greater than you, then chances are you feel empty to life, or maybe you're still wondering what life is about. So pick yourself up and throw yourself where you want to be.

The only part you should give up on is the part that keeps letting you down and the part that keeps giving up on you. The part that makes you feel you don't have what it takes. The part that keeps pushing you down, laughing at you when you try. You have a chance to laugh back, but will you? It's been said that life is 10 percent of what happens to you but 90 percent of what you do about it.

Wow, look at how much fight you got to put back in to win. It's all a process; are you willing to go through it? The moment you apply yourself back to life, it automatically starts to shape and help you form a way for you. In this process, you get the chance to redeem, restore, and restart what you want out of life. If your life is truly important to you, I'll say to you do these three things:

1. *Know what you want.* There must be something you see you believe you can achieve. You've seen it once before, and it's still in you. Write it down. Write the process how you see it. Things go better for you when you write the plan out. Before a home or car is built, they draw out how it's supposed to look before they start the process of building.

2. *Pray for what you want.* Prayer is your way to let GOD know what you have come up with, so he can help you achieve the idea. Big dreams don't happen overnight nor as fast as you think them. So prepare to take the steps necessary to make it come true. Prayer also allows you to get shortcuts, secrets, and more to where you are going. It gives you insight to people and situations better, so you don't waste time in places not needed in life. You have various ideas to lubricate the substance of dreams. No one wants a dry dream. So live life and find things to spice it and make it

fun for you and others. Pray over your dream, family, journey, and success.

3. *Reach out and grab what you desire.* This is not the easiest thing to do, but it is doable. It's all about how strong your belief is. If you believe you can do it, then pull it together to make it happen. Look, you are reading my first book because I believed I could write what I saw and felt. It took me two years to complete. Not worried about my past nor what people have to say about me. Funny thing is, many who talk about you wish they could do or had something you have. So don't be discouraged with the talk—embrace it. You are striving to become something more. You are moving, and they are not. You are changing your story for better, so let it be your motivation to get there.

Can you feel that you have what it takes to grab what you see internally and make it visible? When you start to grab that thing, your past will call you many, many, many times, but if you find the one voice in you that says keep going forward, you will keep breaking the chains off your life. I can tell you all that I want, but only I can make this happen. It's November 2020. I still have people calling me to fix their cars, but I have made a decision to write my book and speeches.

That means I choose to head in a different direction. There are plenty of mechanics out here. I loved it, but what was truly on the inside of me was not being fed, and I was unsatisfied with life and myself. This thing just kept knocking and knocking in me. I know many don't understand what I was going through at the time, but I'm glad I listened to the knock and opened the door. I feel better. I'm at peace within now. It's okay to change your profession due to passion. Follow the thing that makes you happy on the inside. When you find what you want, stick with it. It starts as a crumb, but you have the opportunity to turn it into a loaf of bread.

When we look at the word *potential,* the next word that comes to mind should be *ability.* So when someone says you have potential, they're basically saying you have the ability to do something.

The ability to become a great singer. The ability to become a great husband or wife. The ability to become wealthy, rich, or successful. *Potential is something unseen but has the ability to be seen.* A young football player doesn't play ball hard but has the ability to take it to the next level. An actress doesn't get the role they wanted because they didn't put their all into it.

Many times we lose out because we let certain fears stop us, or we allow others to cast their fears upon us. "No more." Say it with me. "No more." Fear is removable energy. The way you do it is practice where you are going regardless of your thoughts of it. Do it enough until it's in you. We all strive to be different. The only way to do so is not the clothes you wear, the car you drive, or any material stuff. It's all in the vision you see. Your difference comes with the work you put in to get there. The work you put in is the story you are building to even sound different when you get there.

You need to put all focus on it, even on your job, by thinking about it. Practice it on others; prepare yourself. When a baby comes out of the womb, it has the potential to be many things. It becomes more of what it is exposed to most. Look out for potential killers. They are dream killers; they shoot your dream down because they don't see themselves doing it. So they feed you negative thoughts that don't feed you but rob you of your stuff. There's only one thing you can do and that's to prove them wrong.

CHAPTER 9

....

Transitions in Progress

Most of us think we are doing something to transition our life, when we haven't seen any results. Let's talk about when this process starts to take place. Once you get a made-up mind on what it is you actually want, things in life shifts toward what it is. Rather, your mind is changing for good, useful purposes or bad. You are a magnet; you have positive and negative energy in you. It's soulfully on you which way it lands or lead.

A transition is a system of changes that happens once a decision is made. Many people are afraid of change. Change is not bad as long as you direct it the correct way. Every second we change our thoughts and movement, which are not bad changes because they didn't harm us at all. Notice when transition occurs, the world around you changes also. Most of your toughest challenges come from change. It gets tough on you because you have to get out of your normal.

Everything about you, from inside you to the way you appear to others, is shifting and must shift with the transition. It's important this happens because it's part of the character. If your character is not right, the change of transition will not last long, or it will not happen as expected. Maybe you want to stop drinking, smoking, cursing, speeding, or whatever it is. Know you will be tested, challenged, and pushed away from and all. Once you decide to let certain things and people go, it's like battling an addiction. Change isn't easy—letting go of what you're used to if your mind isn't there yet.

So until your brain processes that the transition is happening, you will repeatedly do what you want not to do. Many times we say to God, "Remove whatever it is out." When the feeling is gone, we forcefully intake the habit. Why? Because it's our normal. Over time, we have grown attached to stuff, and it's hard to let go. Think about how much time it takes to develop a habit. Does it take the same amount to quit? No, it doesn't.

It's more so a mind thing. We have a say so about the things we allow in and out of our lives. The big thing about it all is people have gotten too tired to quit. To create a new transition or change for yourself, all you need is a made-up mind, that's all. I said so many times, "I'm done drinking," that I believe God may have gotten tired of hearing it himself.

It wasn't easy for me to do, but once I made up my mind, one day no drink, two days no drink, a week no drink, and so on and so forth. The same thing with smoking Black and Mild. I made up my mind to stop no matter what society had to say. A made-up mind can and will shatter habits and fear. A made-up mind is strong like love; now that's huge.

We all have and had people we love and tried to help, but the best help we could give was to leave them alone. Think about how hard it was to make your mind up before you said forget it. You didn't stop loving the person just because it seemed like it wasn't getting anywhere. The same with our life; we have to see what is working and what isn't. Kick out the unhealthy and invite the healthy. Transition is like when people go to the gym; they don't get results in one day.

Results come once all the hard work is put in days, weeks, and months of working out. If you take this same method and apply it to your vision, after days, weeks, and months of hard work and building, you will get results. Along the time waiting on results, you gain a sense of patience. Big dreams don't happen overnight. Really, your patience should be spent learning and refining to better the vision or dream.

I know it's hard because the world we live in now is so micro-waved. Everyone wants stuff to happen right now. Everyone around you seems like they are doing things faster than you; they are really not. Everyone is just receiving another piece to connect to the puzzle. The way you are looking at them, they see it happening for you and not the same way for them, when everyone should only focus on where they are, where they are going, and what it's going to take to get there.

Seems like GOD blessed the other person and not you; I call this a mirror effect. It's when two images look at each other and each appears to be moving faster than the other, but in reality, they are moving at the same pace. Yes, some people do get there before you, but you don't know when they started nor how far along they have gotten. It's not wise to race to your destiny with anyone. The best way is to set your own pace, and go at your speed; no need to mess up your ingredients.

To a person who does not cook with their heart, food usually don't taste like much. When that passion is there and you give time to marinate, now you are about to shuffle some taste buds. The human is designed to be a godlike mind, which consists of peace, love, joy, happiness, caring, and all those good things that make a person feel whole and complete. You should always think highly of yourself. Set goals to meet your time frames.

In school, they taught us about setting goals, but I didn't under-stand what was being taught to me nor why. Now I'm here in my life, and the goals help to achieve the mission. Goals are very essential to the life of what you desire. They are your preplanned ideas. They are your vision and dream with steps to be completed and mapped out. They are part of your directions to your treasure.

Write out how you see it from the beginning to the end. This is how GOD finishes before he starts a well-thought out process. Same as I said once before about cars and builders—they draw out what it is supposed to look like first, then they go and build. It all will happen easy and fast if you discipline yourself correctly. Transition is not just something we can sometimes just jump up and do. Some things you have to wing yourself off. Sometimes you have to let go cold turkey. The knowing what you want will determine what is and what is not for you.

One thing I will say is, *"You can do it. Stand up for what you deserve. Accept no defeat. If you ever feel defeated, it means go back and rework the plan. Every time you go back to rework it, you will get little stronger. So what if it don't feel right in the beginning? Change/transition never does. Think about the time you had to find a new job."*

I remember how it felt like yesterday. Your mind says, *I don't want to do this, but the bills got to get paid and babies got to get feed.* You have thoughts like, *I'm about to go back home, over a friend's house, or anywhere to take my mind away from this.*

It's stressful. Never let your mind determine your limitations and ability to find what you want and need. No one can or will do what is needed for you. You and only you know where you want to go. You and only you know what it takes to get there. Walking into who I'm becoming now, I didn't let anything get in my way. I was driving trucks and working at Burger King at the same time. Never get too high and feel like you can't work in a lower place. Think of it this way—you are only passing through. Some places you run into in life are just stepping-stones, but people get stuck at a place too long and settle. GOD puts you in places to help you develop the growth you need, but if you are rejecting the lesson, you will never get there. This is how the people of Israel spent forty years in the desert. Life is about growth; I can't say it enough. If you are not growing, it's possible you are one of those in the desert.

Stop the lazy thinking. Pull the positive out, get in your mind, *I'm about to get what I want no matter what. I deserve better. I've been through enough.* Once you get your mind made up on this transition in progress, be open, be willing, and be committed. Make some rules and guidelines like companies to keep yourself on the path of the road of your choice. Remember, no one started at the top, everyone started not knowing everything or anything about where they are going. They all had to sacrifice the time. Enjoy the journey.

CHAPTER 10

....

The Forming of Language

We use words like they are made just to get a point across. They are more than that. I am guilty of this. I never knew how much power I had through my tongue. I didn't read the Bible growing up even though I was introduced to the church. We have to be very aware of the words we use toward others and ourselves.

You know God spoke the things of this world into existence. Just go read the first book and chapter of the Bible. That alone tells us that there is power in words. Not just power in words but also power in tone. The way you give the words meaning. Words are so powerful; they can form how a person turns out to be if they are called something by someone. Words can also beat a person down or build a person up. Think about a time you were feeling bad and someone said something that made you feel better, joyful, and happy.

The wrong words can be more depressing, stressful, and painful if not used correctly. Many times, you have people that joke around a lot and use words for play. Let's look at something from the Bible about the way we should use our tongue. Take time to read over these few verses: *Psalm 34:11–15, Proverbs 15:1–4, Proverbs 18:20–21, James 3:4–8, and Peter 3:8–16.* They all instruct us how we should use our tongue to speak. Many times I've spoken some negative things, and they came to pass. Words are also openers and closers of doors.

Now let's look at how language is built a bit. Say a toddler is with their parents and the parents use foul words all the time. The toddler brain picks up on how parents talk; vice versa with using good words also. Okay, now look at where you are heading. What type of language do they use? Look at some great individuals that are in certain professions. How do they talk? Do they think questions through before answering? Do they speak with a tone of aggression or politeness? Do they speak with words from the heart with respect or disrespect?

Many things have to be looked at and thought about if you are planning to take on the role. There's another language you should consider learning also; it's called body language. This is kind of a crazy one because sometimes people give off the wrong vibe. What I'm saying is, their mind is in one place but body movement is saying something else, which sends the wrong signals. So it's best to always ask questions to have a clear understanding of what's really being interpreted.

Body language is important because say you get a car and someone gets in the car with you. You want to know what kind of mood they are in. Look at the way they have their hands. If their hands are in a fist form, chances are they have some anger built up or some type of tension. Maybe not toward you but toward something. You could ask in a polite way, "Is everything okay?" If you ride with your fist balled up, pay attention to how much in deep thought you are about something that is bothering you.

Now on the flip side of this, if their hands are not in a fist style, chances are they are in some type of peace of mind. If someone immediately puts their hand on their forehead, chances are they are sad and again something is bothering them. So that's just a little to tell you about body language and how important it is to pay attention to it. Being able to read people's body language is a great way to notice what type of mood they are in and how to approach them.

Think about how a person looks to the police when he/she is pulled over and that person keeps twitching, moving, and looking very suspicious. So body language is a giveaway. My point is to make sure you are giving off the right signs to where you are heading. If something is bothering you, find a way to resolve it so you give off the correct signal. For where you are, there are a few levels I'll give you to understand:

1. *Inexperience* which doesn't mean you are not experienced. This is for people who are new to the game. They know little about it. Because you are inexperienced doesn't mean you don't belong at the top. It means you are on your way. Keep up the good work; you started the process.

2. *Good experience* which is what you've been doing enough to answer some questions about it now. You've been through the process of getting some stuff wrong. Now you're on a level of understanding what it really costs to get there. You are in the stages of learning the ins and outs.

3. *Pro experience* is when you are professional enough and have done enough research to be on you own. You can just about teach whatever it is in you. You make it to this level, you are on the market. Now be a competitor.

4. *Fully experienced* which means you've owned your own for a while. Now you can teach the ins and outs on levels you couldn't before. You are skilled and knowledgeable enough to start classes. When you made it here you have met the destiny of a thing. You did a tremendous job. Make sure when you're teaching the ones behind you coming up that it's a true struggle to get to where you are, but with the right attitude about yourself, you can make anything happen.

With these four levels, know that every level will equip you with the language you need for the area you are heading. Prepare yourself with more wanting to understand than wanting to just get there or get done. One more piece of language I want to put with this is the way you dress.

When a person is going to a nightclub, they put on nightclub clothes. When someone is going on a date, they put on date clothes. Not everyone because some people dress one way. I think you get the point I'm making with that, but you must be dressed for where you are heading. You will be amazed how clothes impact you heading somewhere. Think how differently you feel when you just throw on some clothes versus when you take time to put something on you to feel special in. I know when I dress up, I feel renewed, refreshed, and like that's what fits me. I can be dressed up and only have $5 in my pocket and still feel just as important as if I had a few hundreds. I feel different when I put on street clothes and have the same $5.

When I'm dressed for where I'm heading, it makes me feel like people want to know who I am. Kind of important, I guess. The way I speak, think, and feel is quite different because I'm not in my usual comfort zone. When you dress for where you're going, it heightens your sense to be and feel important. When you speak from now on, you should be talking like you are already there. You should be dressed like you are already there. Your mind should always feel like it's in the place because you are pulling it to you with your actions also. The truth is, you should feel that you are already there. Get your language together to pull the crowd in. Remember, you are already there. Set up the stage, the scene of you, so you can see what you are missing. Go get what's yours. It belongs to you.

You know every day we wake up, we have a fresh start to a better, greater, livable life. Why have we not taken advantage of the everyday chances? Are we insane, naïve, or maybe subconsciously we want better out of life but don't do nothing to improve it? We go to the same job and put up with the same BS every day. How do we start our day? Do we even speak to ourselves? Many of us say that's crazy to talk to ourselves when actually, you should be your own motivation first. Speak some power over your life. I found this to help me in most cases. *"I am great, I feel great, I will meet my goals, I will better my situation, and this is not where I will end up. I deserve to wake up and have bills paid. I deserve to wear some of the finest fabrics. I deserve to ride a nice car. I deserve to have a nice annual salary."*

How did that make you feel just reading it in your mind? Felt good, huh? Well, imagine how it would feel if you get up and start your day with a positive vibe. Yes, I know negativity will try to kick in, but you have the power to not let it interrupt your day. So expect negativity to come because you're going against how the world is built. Think about the law of gravity. What goes up must come down. Even when you feel good, the resistance of the world will try to use this law to pull you back to feeling down, oppressed, depressed, and stressed.

You know there is a lot of power in words. Not only that but the way you deliver them also plays a role, as I said early on. My lady and I have a playful relationship, so one day, she said something to me and put *boy* on the end of it. I took offense at it because I felt like she was degrading me. Later that day, we talked about what happened.

She said, "Your friends call you boy."

I had to explain the difference. When my friends say it, it comes off as, "Boy, you a fool," as if it's in a joking manner. Not something like "Get my food, boy," which is a slave-like way.

She was just playing, and I knew it but, I heard it differently. So be mindful and watch how you say it when you say it. You have to come off the way you want to be responded to. You say something aggressive to me, it's a ten out of ten chance you're going get to an aggressive, "WHAT."

Always practice uplifting words for yourself, and it will rub off on others. You can bring beauty to your life just by the words you choose daily. When someone asks how you're doing, I bet you give the same boring, "I'm okay." Change it to, "I'm great," like you mean it, and it's possible you will uplift their spirit with the energy.

Never let anyone determine how you feel on the inside by answering poorly. Even when you feel bad, still reach down and bring some type of enthusiasm out. Start talking like you are great, walking like you're great, and living like you're great. *One last thing. The way you speak your words have to be confident and never arrogant.* There is a very thin line between the two, and people get me mixed up with being arrogant a lot, but I am very confident about myself. It's hard for me to feel less than the way I feel about myself.

CHAPTER 11

....

A Win with Confidence

How many of you are lacking this one piece to the puzzle? You feel something or see something on the inside of you. You need help to proceed to make it happen. When you get to the point of making it happen, you're creating space for you to be next up. Yep, I've done it. When you see or hear the word *confidence*, think of words like *belief, believe, doer, action, self-push,* and *practice.*

These are some of the closest words associated with confidence. How do we help put confidence in someone? How do we get their belief system working again? One way is to understand what a person fears and why. It's just as simple as reversing the fear. Stand on what you fear. Do it because you need to get it out of your system. Fear has stopped a lot of people from doing what they want, even me.

But if you can turn around what's stopping you, then you're on to it. I look at fear for what it was—an invisible feeling that was taking over my life. I've learned that all the *Greats* have had fear before they do what they do. But the thing that separates us is they do it anyway to silence the fear. It's normal; every human has been to a place in their life they feared something and didn't try it. *Key word being normal.*

This whole project is getting out of normal and changing our story to one where we win or fight to win at the end. Fear is your biggest fight and greatest enemy. It stops you from making progress in life. It helps promote procrastination, which you and I don't feel good knowing something and being afraid to do it. That's a lack of trust in ourselves that we can do something. I fought this problem many years and still it's here to this day. Now I find myself doing more of what I want than not because I figured out the problem.

One of the biggest things was that I feared how my friends would look at me and that I would lose cool points, if that's what we still call it. Truth is, once I started doing what I felt was fulfilling to me, I became a game changer. I never knew manhood/womanhood had levels to it. I've learned for a man to step in his manhood fully, he must step on what's in him. He must bring out who he is within. Meaning he must recreate himself so he can live in his truth and stop living the lie that society has fed us forever. *That's deep because before he can recreate, he must recognize he is living a lie first.*

To do this, take a survey of your past five years. What have you really accomplished? Life is about growth. Have you grown mentally, physically, or spiritually? Time is up. Stop running around the same mountain. As a boy, I wrote poems to girls, never knowing that one day I would be writing a book. Just think about that for a second; never realizing what I had in me as a child and now at thirty-five years old writing on a different level.

I learned I had a gift a long time ago, but for the purpose of the gift, God had to let me live out on the limb a bit. So when he was ready to show me what I had, I could have some things to work with. Funny, he never left me even though I cursed at him and called myself walking away from him. God still came to my rescue. *Why?* He knew me. He knew I would do this at this time in my life. I want to say something else, but it would be off course on the subject. So I had to get away from my familiar and I didn't do it on my own. It's crazy how I got here. In the moments of the getaway, I have been in God's training camp.

When I was in this state of mind or place, I was practicing my gifts and talents. Along the way, I had many thoughts about family, friends, and strangers about how I would look doing this. Remember, I come from poverty. I could've been dead or in jail or still in fear. My family is poor, but I was chosen to do something. I heard the voice and answered it. I conversed a lot with God on this journey because it's new to me, even though I felt on the inside my mind still wasn't there.

So what happened was people (family and friends) started calling my phone out of nowhere. I was having these conversations, and there I was performing my gift not even knowing it. Some of this stuff I can't explain. Then I was told to start writing on a topic. I did and another came and another one. I'm not going to go all the way in detail, but this is how the idea of writing a book came about. I had to believe I could and be confident enough that this is what I'm supposed to do.

So here I am telling you, I took a shot at life and you're reading chapter 11. You do the math. It took God to open my mind wide enough. When I started, I didn't have a huge support system. Just my girl, mom, and auntie cheering me on. I was afraid, scared, terrified, and so much more you couldn't imagine, but I was broken and rebuilt by God for his purpose.

Fact: Take it how you want to.

I was telling them about what was happening to me. There was enough pain that I cried sometimes, and my cheerleaders didn't know I did. Once, I got to a point where I felt that God had brought me back from all the tripping I was doing. The next step was to face the real world with what I had. I didn't go straight out there with my gift because it took too much to get it. The cost is great enough that I will cherish it with no abuse. However, one day I was told to build a podium. I got my son to help; it was fun.

Once we finished building it, he said, "Dad don't ever get rid of this." He's only eleven. I don't think he knew I was going to use it. We did that, and then I bought me a camera. Remember, I was still afraid. At this point, my baby brother had passed. So God challenged me to speak at the funeral. I didn't know what to say, but I prayed about it and asked what I needed to say. *Hey, I'm just telling you what I did.*

After some time went by, I was hit with *what to speak about— vision, purpose, and destiny.* When the day of the funeral came, I was a bit nervous. My name was called to go up. As I walked up there, I thought about how full the room was with just about one hundred people. I got up there with a smile from ear to ear, grabbed the mic, and delivered what was on my paper. Afterward, I got hand claps but that didn't let me know that I touched someone.

Some days went by and my mother called me and told me about how some people contacted her to let her know I had something in me. Then I knew this was it. This is what I will put my time and energy in no matter the cost. Since then I've used my podium and camera to do other speeches. When I get up there, it feels like it's where I belong. Now what if I never got up there to speak? I would've never made it to the next level.

Face whatever it is at all cost. You will get fulfillment every time you face your fears. If you can believe just a little and try, God will help you the rest of the way through. You take a step, God takes a leap for you. It's better to die in your truths than your fears because fears help deteriorate your dream, vision, mentality, and future.

Try to win with confidence. When I think about confidence, I think about when I first started driving trucks. I had a mentor to show me how things go. Now driving, shifting the gears, putting on the signal, and others was easy, but when it came to backing the fifty-three-foot trailer in a hole with two trailers on each side was where it became complicated. Not going to go into all the details of backing up a trailer but currently, I wasn't confident at all.

Nerves everywhere, praying I didn't hit nothing. I was then thinking what have I got myself into because I had a trainer there to make me feel like it was okay, and I could try again tomorrow. Until one day, I was done with training, mentor gone. First delivery. I can't tell you how many times I got out to make sure I wasn't about to hit anything. Funny part is, I wasn't even near the other trailers yet. Look, long story short, as time has gone by, I rarely got out to look. I can now back into any dock anywhere whether it's outside or in a building or it has guidelines or just plain ground. It took time to become confident enough by myself.

So sometimes in life, you have to understand what it is you want to happen and constantly do things to become confident at doing it. You don't become great without believing you are. Analyze what you are doing and where you are going, knowing it's going to take everything you've got to make it happen. Yes, there's going to be ups and downs, but part of the outcome depends on how confident and serious you are about the results you expect.

Don't let anyone rush your greatness. Yes, there are some money-hungry, impatient people. You must always move at your pace, but not so slow that time seems like it is running out all the time. Create a pace that has balance in it. You'll find it's easy to do your thing and enjoy it. It takes time for greatness to form and show itself. That comes with the correct, proper training and preparation. Your confidence of doing what you believe in is just the same as having faith. Know you can choose how far you go in life if you're not tied up with ropes or chains.

Your brain can take you to places you never imagined. Think about it for a second—where you are right now at this very moment reading this book. You thought about it first. Then you went and made it happen. It's the same way with everything else. Yes, hard but mentally, how much fight you got? Confidence has to be there even when you don't feel it. So that means you have to dig deep to find the energy. You can do it.

First, don't tell yourself you can't do it. One other thing, don't let anyone cast their fears on you because they didn't see it for themselves. Relax, take a deep breath. Get this in your head. You are everything you want to be, but you have to be a relentless fighter in bringing out what's yours. Say to yourself right now some things that build you up and really makes you feel good but try not to do it with liquor or weed. Not saying you got to quit your stuff, but I want you to see and feel that you are your own motivator. That's important to your journey, that you know yourself more than anyone.

A lot of people get confidence and arrogance mixed up. There's a thin line as it's been said once before. You must make your own statement about you. I will say arrogance is a bragging-type attitude versus confidence that has a more for sure one. One of my partners looked at me and said, "You think you better than everybody."

I looked at him calmly and said, "No, I don't think I'm better than everybody." I sat there for a sec and came back and said, "You know what, I am better than everybody."

Not ever meaning to bash anyone. Never let someone deprive nor depreciate my value. The way I see me, no one can change that. His reason for saying it was because of my way of doing things. I have a code that I live by, and it's simple: *I can and I will.* Otherwise, I do things that the normal person doesn't do. It's just me being confident about me.

I make sure that I'm doing right by me first and not letting anyone determine where nor how far I go. I never train my mind to say *I can't or ain't.* As long as I have breath in my body, I believe in doing what I feel versus what makes me look cool. Understand these are winner strategies for success. You have to believe you can do whatever it is you want. Hell, I believe you can and will. So what if they don't understand you or say you think too much? So what if they don't feel what you feel? They have to get where you are and do what you do to understand. One lesson before I close—never treat people like you are Mr./Mrs. Big Shot. Help others to get more confident now you know how.

CHAPTER 12

....

Disciplinary Action

Ever wonder how a person with a job that doesn't pay much pays a car note, rent, take care of the family, put food on the table, and still keep a little money in their pocket? They become somewhat good with saving and managing what they had or have. That alone takes some hard decisions. Think about how an athlete becomes well developed in their profession.

To make it simpler, look at how pastors, preachers, or bishops teach the Word of God. All these things I've named have one thing in common—it's discipline. They all have it in order to be who they are. Discipline is a mature mindset that challenges a person's need for growth or to grow. It helps keep people in shape with what they are involved in.

Many of us pray and ask for a car, house, business, etc. When before we ask for these things, we should really ask, "Are we able to handle what we're asking for? Am I ready to take on more? Am I responsible enough to take care of and keep what I'm asking for?"

Before you pray, do you look at how you handle the stuff you already have? The car you drive now—do you routinely care for it? The home you live in—do you keep it clean like you deserve a better or bigger one?

I've been driving trucks now for twelve years. I've been wanting my own truck for twelve years. Here I am now just getting my own truck twelve years later. Why so long? I spent my money recklessly; I had no savings plan. I can go down a whole list of reasons why it took me so long, but to shorten it, I wasn't disciplined or holding myself responsible for getting it done.

No, I'm not complaining, and yes, I finally got one, but look at the time I wasted playing. I can hear someone saying, "GOD took you through that for a reason." No, I took me through that because I was unconscious of my way of living. I was blinded by the fun I was having with friends and drinking. No, not making them take the blame either. I am my own blame because of me being what I called myself "a grown man."

I didn't recognize/realize I wasn't growing mentally. I always wanted to read, work out, and do heathy stuff for my life, but it took me a long time because I was living so loosely. I never gave myself a chance to grow mentally because for one, I thought, *I know enough about life.* I came to find out I didn't know as much as I thought. I let my pride get in the way of asking certain questions. I didn't listen when some people were trying to tell me. I understand now it took time to learn what would help move my process rather than me just doing a whole lot of moving and not making any progress.

I understand I want something bigger than myself, so I have humble myself to the things that will get me there. To do that, I must take responsibility and become disciplined for everything. I must learn and apply. This is not an easy thing to do, but I can do it with a strong mind, a focused mind, a growing, mature mind, and a disciplined one.

When trying to develop and grow mentally to get ahead in life, it is hard work. *Discipline* is a huge word that no one can overlook at no aspect of life, from a drug dealer to the president of the country. You can't make it without it, trust me. I've tried; it's harder without discipline than it is trying to develop it and actually doing it. It's even harder if you're trying to do it without letting some stuff go. You will overwhelm yourself and quit.

Let go of what's not getting you there. Discipline will change your schedule from doing everything to just doing stuff that matters. When you become disciplined to or for something, you give it your time. The more time you give it, the more it grows on you and in you. When you are disciplined, people trust you a little more. You get things done a little faster. Discipline is setting your mind to do something, and no matter what, you make it happen.

Have you ever tried to save a thousand dollars, but it seemed so hard? There is no way possible you can do it. Discipline is putting little by little to the side till you get there. Discipline makes sure everything counts. So it's important to add to what you feel you do have much of. Think about how small things impact the world. Treat goals, dreams, visions, and aspirations like a woman. Small and simple things matter the most. Being disciplined is not easy, but to keep and maintain what you build, it will be well needed.

When you commit yourself to something, find ways to become more responsible in it so you don't lose it. There was a time in my life I wanted a relationship but didn't want to let the single life go. How could I be so double-minded? I wanted to start certain businesses, but I didn't save the money to do so. With things you want to happen, understand what it takes to control yourself in a certain way. Being disciplined is not easy because here comes the sacrifice.

When most people see they have to give up something they love or like doing for something they don't know if it will work is tough. Well, let me ask why you constantly allow the fear of failure and the failure of others control your mind. You have to step out some time and try. You are already disciplined to something or someone. Is it the right thing or the right person? Is where you are where you want to be forever? If not, make your mind up and fight the battle to get where you're going.

Imagine one day looking back on life and saying, "I remember." I remember the journey it took for me to get here, a tough fight but it was well worth it. Imagine being in a peace of mind living your best life rather than living lies about yourself. You are somebody; treat yourself like it. Give your life a meaning. You know I learned it's okay to run from your past, the faults, mistakes, blames, pain, losses, and all. The most important thing about it all is where you are running to.

Imagine a person running in place, going nowhere in the same spot doing the same thing. No progress of going anywhere. Have you been making progress? Are you running to a better life, or are you just running in the same place? All this means is find something you can reach, that you can run to in order to start to run from. I'm running to complete this book. I'm running to build my trucking business. I'm running to get myself in a position to help somebody. Don't just be somebody running and don't know where you are running to. Replace your fear with disciplined confidence. You shall. You can. You will.

One last thing before I close this out. Another thing I learned that helped get this is I had to learn how to live in my corrections rather than my faults. No, I'm not perfect and didn't have the perfect life. Didn't grow up having stuff. Messed up so many times I lost count. Lost a lot alone the way here. Done things I'm not proud of. It all hurt, but the one thing that pushed the hurt away and helped pick me up was I started to correct little by little things about me. I started to not be so angry at the world or GOD because I found the cure was already in me. I just needed to recognize it, so I could start to cure myself of some things.

Then came some other good things. I also learned that even though things looked ugly at the moment, I still had to believe in GOD and that I was doing the right thing by staying positive in my thinking. It's tough to do that in many situations, but to be a true, firm believer in GOD, you have no choice but to keep walking and be thankful. Don't walk around with stuff you can't do anything about. Only focus on what you can control, what really works, what you can grow, what you can get rid of. I believe in you, but that doesn't do any good if you don't believe in you.

CHAPTER 13

The Human Balance Beam

A man's greatest stress, frustrations, depression, and lack of wanting to have more in life is being unbalanced. A woman's greatest anxiety, feeling of oppression, and low output to life is being unbalanced. Both being interchangeable. Life is filled with tangled obstacles; after you make it through one there's another. Seems as if it never stops. Being off balance seemingly can control how far we are willing to go to be successful. Look at all that we juggle daily. Family, work, friends, and habits.

I want to mention self-time, but many of you don't have that. Why? I can't answer this for all, but for some or many even, in our childhood growing up, that wasn't an option unless you were the only child. So I'm saying, we always have had people to accommodate, to fill the room of emptiness our whole life. We were not taught to have time to ourselves. It wasn't something that was thought of as important. When was the last time you spent thirty minutes, one hour, or two hours with just you trying to develop yourself?

I know the Bible says man shouldn't be left alone. People say an idle mind is the devil's playground, but put all that to the side for a moment. What this time allows is for you to think, plan, recharge, and repower. Now many will say I spent this and that amount of time doing that, but was it a quiet and mediating place? I bet you were listening to your favorite music, which there's nothing wrong with that if you are working on bettering you. So many only spend their time with some of the biggest time stealers of our time—Facebook, Instagram, watching pointless TV shows, etc.

This time you make for yourself is supposed to bring you back to the drawing board. From now on, when you get time to yourself, just image or get a writing board and fill it with the things you want to accomplish and have. Write down what you think needs to be adjusted and things you think will help you become a better person. You got what you want to do; also you have family and friends. Of course you have work; you will always have that.

Let's try to put some things into perspective. To balance these, acknowledge what's most important to least important. So let's say we have the typical family setting—wife, husband, children, friends, dreams, and self. Every day from now on, get self on point enough to focus on everything else that could possibly pull energy from self. So wake up, self—need to pray and get an understanding of the daily goals for responsibilities self-handled daily. If necessary, write the plan how you see it.

Now everything's not going to go how you expect every time but to have a plan is major and helps a lot. Every day self needs to find something that can keep self in a positive mood so things can flow better. And when problems come, you don't get overthrown by the problem, you overthrow it. So self has to create time for self to potentially balance at a better level.

Sometimes you need to have lunch and dinner by yourself away from home. You will begin to see and acknowledge that sometimes, this is all you need to make it through many things. To get unlocked, unstressed from under some of the pressure to handle life better daily, spend some time digging within to get real answers to the problems you face. Pressure builds up a lot throughout life. Many times we don't release it—how are we supposed to?—and many times it's too late.

The time you get to yourself can be refreshing according to how you spend it. Ever since I've been writing this book, at the end of the day I leave with a nice smile on my face because I'm actually doing something that satisfies me internally. I feel even if I never sold one copy, at least I got it out of me. I'm doing what drives my ideas to build upon one another, and certain stuff I write helps me to see the potential I have.

What if I never did this? Maybe I would feel congested or that type of way. I know what it feels like to try to fulfill something in you, and it seems like nothing is working. I was that person. Back on subject before I get off too far. Now in this refreshing time, you should be able to figure out bills, family, friends, dreams, and habits. You should be able to think things through a little better. You will recognize what you can do and what you need help with. It gives you time to draw up a plan and handle most things. Just an example:

- Wake up
- Prayer and alone time
- Listen to positive messages
- Breakfast for the family
- Work
- Home discussion—what the day was like for everyone
- Family fun time
- Have drink with friends
- Pray with the family
- Alone time again
- Bed

I do not know what it might look like to you, but this is something to help you balance a bit. If you are a busy person, maybe you can set it up like this: "No matter what, I'm spending two hours with wife or husband, one hour playing with kids, and maybe forty-five minutes with the friends." Like I said, I don't know, but we have to be more considerate about how we use our time toward life. No matter what, every day spend at least an hour and a half on what you think will make you successful. This is how the Greats, people who are becoming great, and you, will develop the strengths needed to conquer and overcome the challenges to where you are heading—by simply spending time learning it.

Being balanced is just having things in order enough that life does not stress you. When you learn how to balance everything, you introduce yourself to a healthier lifestyle. Look around you, and look closely to see how unbalanced some people are. Now look a little closer to see how and what you need to do in order to live a more balanced life. When it's balanced, you handle problems better. When you get it balanced, fight to keep it that way because on the flip side, you are letting an early death creep in. Balance brings laughter, brightness, and good feelings that you can accomplish many things. It brings great attitude to life. The more you accomplish, the better you feel.

Too many people live a boxed life. Set that person on the bench coach and get better with balance. Unbalanced looks like an alcoholic that doesn't know their limit. Every time they drink, they end up falling all over the place. Balanced is the person that has a stopping point to assure he/she doesn't go over the limit to still be functional. Balance is like when you season food exactly right. It is also being able to get in touch with who you are on the inside.

To be aligned with your divine source is huge and where you want to be. This brings so much completion to life. This is the point where you satisfy your wants and desires. Many people have a problem with showing who they are internally. That's bad because that keeps us kicked out and stepped on by our true wants and desires. My dad asked me one time what is true happiness. Of course, being in my early twenties, I answered wrongly.

Take a second and ask yourself what true happiness is. The way you live right now, are you truly happy? Where you are in life right now, are you straight? Do you feel as if you have gotten all that life has to offer you? Be truthful with who you are. You are hiding behind your habits, claiming you are happy when on the inside you're about to blow. On the inside, you feel less than what you can or should be. That was me before I knew how to balance, but never again will I live that lie.

Let me answer the question a little for you. True happiness is when you can live your means of life. Meaning the things you think about at the core of you. True happiness is when you can look back at life and you can honestly say you are proud of how it turned out. True happiness is growth. When we can go within ourselves and correct the wrongs. True happiness is when we can step out on faith and manifest ourselves to the world no matter the cost. So to sum it up, it's a feeling of satisfaction from your trial-and-error moments. You must go back and complete those tests and stop running.

We are so clingy to acting according to how others want us to rather than how we feel on the inside. So balance will not ever come to you because you put more of you toward what others want and see you as than what you truthfully want for yourself. So many people have adjusted to the way people want to see them rather than how they see themselves. Just start sitting and observing; you'll see a lot. So yes, I'm saying a lot of people are living a lie. This eats a person alive. People are caught up in what's cool to the world rather than manifesting themselves to the world and becoming the coolest.

There are more trend followers than self-manifesters. We need more self-manifesters to balance. It takes time to get the balance needed for what you are trying to live with and become. The balance that it truly needed requires the figuring out of time, system, strategy, and cost. Great people put their selves on a schedule to balance their life diet with what they are trying to accomplish.

Once you get the balance, you will become a letdown to someone because you now focus on the stuff that matters to you. For so long they depended on you, but now they can't reach you. That's totally okay. If it's not growing with you, it's growing away from you. That's supposed to happen. See, you need balance, so anything that's not moving with it becomes deadweight to the journey. So it has to fall off. You are balanced. You can level things out, so get your head in the game because life is about to change.

CHAPTER 14

....

Expectation Season

In order to expect anything of this world and the next dimension, you have to do one or two things. You must plant something to get something. When a tiny seed is planted, we get trees, vegetables, fruits, plants, bushes, and unimaginable success—from the time we put the seed where it needs to be, to the time it sprouts out or up to create the mindset that I'm waiting for something to happen. If you never planted anything, you will not and should not be looking for anything. A pregnant woman expects a baby in nine months because someone has planted a seed in her. Dogs, cats, bears, spiders, rats, and all can expect something if a seed is planted. However, seed planting can come in many forms. Planting a seed is just the same as putting in a request.

When we pray, we put in a request. When we fill out applications, we put in a request. You tell someone to do something, you put in a request. Now on the flip side of what you requested, you expect certain things to happen. It is amazing to me how we plant stuff and get results. It's almost like magic, but it's also the work you have to put in behind what you plant. When planting, we must make sure we are planting in the right season. Not only that but planting in the right type of soil and planting the right product.

This all comes to what you are putting in you to push out of you. The stuff we feed our mind, body, and soul—is it healthy? Have we cleaned ourselves mentally, spiritually, and physically to intake what we trying to do? There's nothing wrong with many things that people try to make sound bad. The question is, are you in control of you enough that what you hear, eat, drink, and see doesn't affect you?

Seeds are some of strongest raw minerals here on earth. That's why you must not be afraid to try something new or an old idea. Look at how much one tiny seed can grow—how much it produces and reproduces. Think about what a seed goes through for it to be so small. Seeds are planted; they become all these amazing things. It's okay for you to dream bigger than what you think you can do. How do they remain confined to what they are designed to produce? GOD created seeds and spoke to them and told them this is all you are to be. GOD also spoke to us and said we are to be conquerors of many of our thoughts.

We are designed to be multitalented, but it stops when you stop. Pick up something that you would be proud to say you are attached to. Let's think about how you plant negative seeds in your life. They don't do anything; they are not prospering to your future nor present. They do exactly what they are supposed to do and that's to be a bad influence for your life and that's all it will ever be. Hold up. But you, on the other hand, are what you think you are. Not saying every moment will be good or bad.

I had my own moments of bad-influenced negative thoughts and still have them from time to time, but I control the outcome all the time. To think about how unhealthy a person is on the inside due to negative thoughts, that had to have been planted for years. This must be dealt with so the seed you see that's so beautiful and all that can out. New seeds have to be planted, and the great thing is, you don't have to wait for a season. You can start now. Start putting in good thoughts. Speak great things over yourself, family, and children. Eat the good, talk the good, walk the good, and listen to the good.

Society has brainwashed too many negative self-hate types of people when all that needs to be done is just a little more than what you've been doing. Put out a little more energy than you normally put out. I know you heard misery loves company. The company for misery is only more misery. If you are not a miserable person, stop indulging yourself in and with it. You are now on a new level. You don't need to function on low levels anymore. Practice a higher class, live a higher class. Remember, beware of the seeds you plant. When you plant seeds, you take care of what you plant. Seeds grow with water, dirt, and care. People grow into things by being involved with that which it is the watering.

We must be mindful of what we water within us. Keep in mind—important things get water only. Everything else can be bypassed. You know the most frustrated, stressed, and depressed and so on and so on people are people with no growth. A seed that does not grow is in the wrong environment; once it's placed in the correct one, it can grow and reproduce like it's supposed to.

You stretch in life by growing in life. That is the only way you just about guarantee longevity. What this means is *manifest you to be a less stressed you*. Things can't grow or move without you putting in the effort. Effort requires action from the body to do research and make sure you are moving in the correct direction. You know when you are going somewhere, it should become noticeable to you about hitting the same bumps in the road because you keep taking the same path, making the same dumb mistakes, and looking for a different outcome.

Let me ask you a question. "Why haven't you tried a different route yet?" Yes, there will be more bumps along the way of the new route, but guess what, you just changed your scenery. You just opened yourself up to a mind of exploring. Long story short, do not just live life going down only roads you know. Take a detour somewhere. You'll maybe find there's a quicker way if you just detour, explore, and stay the course.

The moment you start to release some stuff is the very moment you should expect something to come. Always remember, nothing comes easy. Work must be put out in order to receive what's expected. When you expect something, ask yourself, "What are you expecting?" Are you looking for something good or bad? What did you do to expect it? Remember the saying is *you reap what you sow*. What did you put out there to come back? With applying the right substance to your life, you can expect a good turnout. I am a believer that when you do good things, good things follow and come back.

You have sex with no condom, you can expect a baby. You pour gas on something and light it with a match, you can expect a fire. You slap a gorilla; chances are you better run for your life. You go to work; at the end of the week, you expect a check. What are you doing to preserve the expectation of where your life should be? Right now, are you a dependent or are you dependable?

A dependent gets filed on someone's income taxes. Being that someone supplies what you need and maybe never what you want nor to expect. Stop giving people dominion over you. That tells me exactly what you want—a sorry, regretful, frustrating, pathetic, stressed, depressed, and oppressed life. On the flip side, being dependable is far greater to be able to do for yourself. To be able to learn what is needed so you can prevail in life. No one should have to make you want to do better. No one should have the power to think for you if you are functional and within your right mind.

Many times, I have been in various conversations whereas I hear the same basic saying, "I'm tired and at the peak of giving up." So let us raise a question. Have you exhausted all you can do in order to take your life to the next level, or have you settled as a dependent of society?

Read these next few words very closely; repeat if you have to. No one is going to give you s——; you need to make a way. You must go get what you think you deserve. Whether it's reading the instructions on how to bake biscuits or reading the dictionary on expanding your vocabulary, you can't expect much if you are not trying to grow the thinking of your mind. What is it that you expect from you? I expect to become one of the greatest writers of all time and one of the greatest life changers.

I've been praying, writing, reading, and listening because I expect something different of me. I know how it feels when you fail yourself once and over and over; it then becomes okay, but it's not because you wing yourself into not trying anymore. I've done it many times, but I didn't settle for that because I felt something in me that wouldn't let me go. Now I will not let it go. So if you are at the brink of giving up, let me say I am a success overcomer of all life dealings. Listen to me—you can be and you are the same. Dig deep, deep, deep down, and find that fighter in you. Not to harm someone but fight for yourself. Say, *"I am a winner, I am a champion, I am greatness, I am a child of God, I deserve to be on top, and I will become who I am destined to be."*

After those few affirmations, how do you feel? Look for no help; you must do it your way first. Feel good about the journey; it's the best want to travel. Plan the journey; know you have control over it. Fight your way up through as a seed. Know everything is against you. Pray it off; you ask for forgiveness of your sin and move forward.

You have to invite GOD in to fully win. As a matter of fact, start expecting the change that's about to come. One thing that will happen to you whether you want it or not is change. But what are we changing to is the hugest question that you should ask yourself. Start living your life like you've already got it.

I had a steak party in an apartment because I expected to do it on a larger scale someday. See, when you know what you're planning, then you know how to grow, where to grow, and what you're growing. You plant tomato seeds, fertilize, and water…expect tomatoes.

So the formula is simple; it just has to be applied. Expectation can become one of the greatest things that can happen to you in life if you are expecting. I didn't think I could do a great job on this subject, but I prayed and asked GOD to grab my pen, and I believed he did in writing this book, so I expect it to come out great.

CHAPTER 15

Being Responsible Cost

When I see the word *responsible*, I see the word *ownership*. Ownership means it's in one's possession. When you have something in your possession, you take ownership for something that's in your possession. So if you let me borrow your car, it's in my possession, and if the car comes back with a new scratch or dent on it, I'm responsible for the damage to the car. Responsibility goes farther than that when you're trying to live, start, or accomplish dreams, visions, and goals.

The part we must really consider is that the idea belongs to us to bring to life, and it takes a lot of courage to go through all steps required. Look how sometimes it's difficult to be a parent that is responsible for a child who doesn't understand where they are trying to go; you may have been there already. The mistake falls back on the parenting depending on the age of the child. In life today as we know it, there are very few people who want to take on responsibility.

Some can't handle the pressure when things go bad. They sometimes lack the knowledge of what to do, and others just don't want any responsibility at all. No matter if you want it or not, you are responsible for something as long as you live in this world, universe, and dimension—whether it's just walking the kids to school or wherever you land in life. It's easy to start but a hard thing to finish. Think about what it takes to carry more stuff on your back with everything you already have and it not just being for you. Once you understand what they are, understand there are good characteristics in being responsible. The more responsible you become, the more people trust you with things and positions.

When you are committed to things you are responsible for, you then become a protector for that. God is responsible to make sure you get to your destiny, so he will protect you at all cost to get you there. God will not and cannot get you there if you are afraid to step out on faith and not be obedient when he tells you to stay, stop, or go. You have to become disciplined to everything that revolves around it. You will not let anything violate it. If you do, then you could lose it. When you give someone your word, you are taking responsibility for something. If the bond is somehow broken and it's your fault, no matter how much you say you are good, deep down, you feel you let yourself down and others.

So let's not continue to practice being a failure of our word and trust. You know, being responsible simply says, "I'm going to stand up for what I believe in. I will not hear and believe negative stuff that tries to keep me from conquering where I'm heading and what I'm building." You can pat yourself on the back when you stay true to what you committed to.

The greatest cost of responsibility is sacrifice. I say this because it's hard to give up on things when you are comfortable. If you want the better life you're thinking about, comfort has to be broken. You must get comfortable trying to make the impossible possible. Sacrifice comes into play in a lot of decisions that have to be made. When you want to go somewhere in life and look at all the things you have to carry alone with you, you also start to see things you can get rid of that will be a slowdown to the mission.

Ask yourself right now, "How can I take some weight off?" The best way to eliminate is to ask yourself, "What is important for my journey?" Only take what is useful. Tough decision-making comes when sacrifice comes into play. Some people have to let go of habits, friends, family, and hobbies. This is painful to do because you are so attached to these things and people. You have grown a bond of love with them, but it doesn't mean you lose the love you have for them because you made a choice to do something with your life. It's hard to separate from the known to walk into the unknown. It's a tough decision. You get feeling and thoughts about, *Am I making the right choice?* because it feels like you are losing something, and you are.

The reality of it is, you are growing into another stage and level of life. You have a choice to stay where you are and be content with what you have, but understand that you are responsible for your personal growth. You have the ability to go beyond where you are. The biggest challenge you face is what you will leave behind. There are many things you can come back to. The very people you think you are leaving need you to do your part, so they could grow. That's deep; think about if you start doing better. The power of you pushing people into growing toward their purpose.

Sacrifice is easy when you believe the place you are going is where you are supposed to be. Many of us have bills and family to care for. We get up, work jobs, and do all types of things to make ends meet. I was a driver for DHL overnight, Burger King worker in the morning, and fixing cars in-between, so I understand what you are going through. I will say you can do it if you want. So I want to help make it a little easier to meet your responsibilities.

So let's say the average person's bills total out to $1,500 a month. Instead of looking at this $1,500 in one whole figure, let's break it down. So there are thirty days in month. How much a day do you need to make in order to reach $1,500 in thirty days? Fifty dollars a day. What is happening here is you have a job but you also find a way to make an extra $50 a day. This will help ease up some financial stress.

Also, it helps to build momentum to start a business. Your $50 a day could double with the right product and customer service. After months, you start to make maybe $3,000 a month in a business you started on your own. It takes time to grow things. I've also learned that a lot of people are afraid of meeting new people. If you can get this thought through your head, which is that person has your money in their pocket, how do you get it into your pocket? You will become responsible for creating the way to get your money from them. It's your responsibility to find stability.

CHAPTER 16

....

Believe What You Are Dreaming

I love to write, and I've stopped driving over the road. So the place where I usually focus and write is gone. That was my place with no distractions, no one to knock on the door, no calls to come help people with daily life problems. Now I'm home. I have all types of distractions. Sometimes I walk in my house and my mind looks for a place to escape, so I found myself putting focus in movies rather than what I really wanted to do. So now I have to decide whether to let my mind be focused on what it wants or find a way to focus.

So here I am today writing because I choose to focus on what's important to me and my vision. See, there are times when you will have down moments and you will feel the Creator is not with you, but the truth is, this is your test to see how serious you are. What's the purpose of helping someone if their attention is not on the task? What good would it be for you to pay for college and you don't learn from what the professor's teaching? Your attention is elsewhere. You must always be aware of what you are doing and most importantly why you are doing it.

You are the most valuable piece of your own puzzle. If you are putting a puzzle together and you don't have a picture to tell you what it is you're putting together, then you are wasting your time. When you want to manifest your dream, there are levels to the vision. Know how far you want to go and be willing at all cost to get there and beyond. Know in your mind there is nothing standing in your way but that inner voice that fights to either keep you down or lift you up.

You control which voice you're fighting with. This little voice is vital to your success. Say you go in a store and you see a sale. You have the money to pay for something, but that little voice tells you, "It's too much. You are going to be broke if you buy that." Shatter the glass thoughts, and buy what you want. How many times have you seen something you couldn't afford? How did you feel when you walked away from it? Not so good, huh? How many times you could have done something about your situation and you didn't? How did it make you feel? Not so good, huh?

So this is your chance to change all that. Stop limiting yourself to society's limitations of what you should have and how far you can go. When you want something to happen, it's a thought first, but along with that thought, you must apply action. Whether it requires reading, watching videos that you once didn't like, or standing in the mirror presenting your product, gaining rhythm and becoming consistent with where you are going will help you get there a bit faster and easier. It makes it easy for the Creator to put you there. Never take your mind off your mission. When it's done, you will know. You will not have an incomplete feeling about it.

To believe in yourself is simply knowing you can do and become what you see within. Remember, no one knows how to nor sees what you are to produce. No matter how many people you see doing it, remember, believing your way could be a greater and easier way for someone else. There will be people that will try to talk you out of what you see. Pay them no mind because they have not submitted to their own vision. Never let someone cast their fears of failure on you because they are afraid to try again, or they let that little voice talk them out of it. If they have submitted to their vision, then they know it can happen, and they will push you.

When you believe, open your mind to all possibilities and maximum capacity to receive and to give all you are supposed to. That will help widen your vision or dream. Believe outside of what you believe in. The universe is set up to help manifest what you are willing to put your time in. To believe means to never give up on what you believe in, even if it means death. Do not let that scare you. Death is a technique used to put fear in you. Fear is darkness. Fear is the absence of courage and confidence.

You must find a positive way to constantly go until you get whatever it is in you out of you because it will eat you alive. Believe, manifest, and conquer your gift. No war or battle is won without putting up a fight, setbacks, losses, ups and downs, and sense of trying to win. You are the sword to your victory. Your victory will come from what you have prepared yourself with before the fight started.

Believe you will have a constant overflow from the Creator because you are doing what you were designed to do. Who can take it away from you? No one. It's your duty to make it happen to accomplish any task set before you with the correct preparation. When you believe, it sets you away from and makes you different from what you once knew. My last words on this is live your dreams, widen your vision, stand on your actions, and believe.

CHAPTER 17

Start to Finish

Time after time, people begin processes that they don't end. This widely creates a disease internally. A silent killer in many communities. One thing I have acknowledged is that some people don't know how to start a thing. Many lack the resources, energy, support, and drive to finish. I can tell you hundreds of stories of me, family members, friends, and others that all suffer from this critical disorder. We plan things out in our mind, and it's so easy there to think it out, but when the director says *action*, we don't go in our role with 110 percent. I can be honest and say I've started lawn services, retail resale businesses, and a host of other things but never followed through.

I started with the same mind frame we all start with. I see the money that can be made off a product or service. After doing it for a while, the money wasn't coming the way I pictured it, so I lost interest. Now that I'm thirty-five, I question myself. "What if I had pushed myself, had someone to push me, show me, or would've told me how or said you're on the right track, don't quit?"

Maybe I would've gotten a whole lot farther a long time ago. Now let's look at the start of a thing. To start something, you must apply yourself. Before you apply, you must know what it is you're applying you to do. What is your ultimate goal? What is it you want to happen? So let's say I wanted to start a car wash business, and I want to grow big enough to give some people the opportunity to work, learn skills, and make some money. So that would be the goal. The very next thing is research and gather supplies.

Now there have been times where I didn't have the money to buy what I needed. So when this happens, you must

1) borrow the money if you have someone you've built a trust bond with; and

2) get a job to support the idea, or you can start another small business that's less costly.

It's okay to want to do something and don't have enough to start. This should create a hunger to get it done. There will be times when it seems like it's just not lining up right. Understand the process is teaching you and strengthening you, so when you get to where you're going, you can handle it. Also, you are creating an overcoming story that someone may be watching you or you will tell to help give them courage, knowledge, and wisdom that they may experience.

Now after you get the supplies, finally you might be thinking, *Now I'm about to go get this money.* Well, the problem you might face is no one knows your work or know you. So how do you get your business booming with all the other car washes around? This is the hard part of starting. The part where I may have always lacked or fell off. With all the supplies and you feeling like if someone just stops to see what I can do. Don't wait on them. Remember you are in the business to grow to your goal. This is where you become more creative than you've ever been before. Therefore, you must step out on the ledge of opportunity and create for yourself. This shows how committed and dedicated you are. This is where you are trying all those amped up ideas to open the door for you. This is where you must apply your energy on the level you see yourself in the future. Take your mind away from where you are.

The drive and energy you put out must be highly impacted with compassion, gratitude, respect, and many more attributes. All these things work together to assemble and align you with God's features and characteristics. Have you seen a person who seems like they are glowing all the time and seems approachable? This what you are creating for you, your brand, and what you expect from others. Another thing I've recognized about many people is that they are afraid to meet new people. They are afraid to talk. We've heard it before, "A closed mouth don't get fed."

You can't reap success by being quiet. As a matter-of-fact, success isn't quiet. You got to be willing to open a portal to succeed. Your mouthpiece and work ethic will show and prove. Now I want to introduce something that is crucial, that we all have at one point or another done. *In the stages of growing, we all have wasted time.* A lot of it is not done on purpose; it's done unconsciously. See, we use our own willpower to do the things we want rather than what is important to our future and self-growth. I've realized that it takes three to six months to change the situation of anyone who is determined enough and willing to evolve to new levels in life to begin the change that is needed to happen.

This comes with pain from growth and pain from the stuff you leave behind but not because you want to but because you have to. Many things that you have outgrown that still pacify your circumstances. Wrap your mind around the time you sit waiting on something to happen can be the same time making something happen. When we are talking about time, we must understand one of the most important principles of time—that it must not be wasted and it must be used productively and wisely.

So now, how do we maximize something that we have much but so little of? The best and quickest answer to that is to apply every inch of thought you have in you and every piece of energy to exercise what I call the time capsule. I know you've seen in movies where people draw pictures and write stuff on paper and in a certain amount of years they go back and check to see did any of it happen. This is you, and your ideas that are in you. You are the time capsule, and you are also the one who can bring it to life. You are also the one who will look back to see did any of it happen. Are you still one of those procrastinators? It's okay that something didn't work but not okay that you think of it and didn't try.

Once again, the silent killer has struck. Something else we must watch out for and it's called a *time thief.* When we set out to become conquerors, achievers, and overcomers, life puts out a hit on you for you not to become no more than whatever that doubting voice tells you. It's high priority that 90 percent of everything you tie yourself to must be conducive to your growth. *As I said early on, we have a lot but little time.*

So that means you must spend time with where you are going such as the environment you are linked to. It's okay to chill with a few friends that are not on the same page sometimes. It's not okay to enjoy your habits that don't fit. The key to what I'm saying is you must understand the law of attachment also. You can be doing your own thing, but be careful because you can start to turn away from your desire to feed someone else's dream and not being conscious of doing your own.

I was fixing on cars, and I wanted to give up and start writing, doing speeches, developing myself, but it seems like I got calls more than ever. So yes, I was trying to work a job, work on cars, and develop myself. Don't get me wrong; I liked to work on cars. I grew a passion for it because I was able to help people and also make extra money. Until one day I lost the passion for it in my spirit. I can't explain how it happened, but I do know God asked me to do something for him. He said to me, "You are a great servant of others, and I have something else for you." So I was called to help on another level.

Immediately, I accepted the mission because I had ran once before for many years. Every time I went to fix a car, I started feeling like I was losing or missing out on something. It was like I wasn't being fulfilled on the same level anymore, and over time, I understood I was called to help on a different level where my gift can be used on a greater level. When I started to fix a car, I was called to help keep the cycle of transportation going for some people who actually didn't have enough to pay a shop.

Where I am in life now with the change is a way greater feeling than ever before. Picture a guy with nothing, struggling to make ends meet but helping everyone he could. Not knowing God was taking him through all that to learn from. In the year 2020, I bought my first semitruck, I've written my own speeches that have been recorded, you are reading my book, and mentoring people. Also I have encouraged many that they can do better just off my actions because they saw me broke. I've been watching the impact God has put on people through my actions, work, and gift.

Me releasing what's inside of me has been one of the greatest things that ever happened to my life. Understand all this took time to develop. To have any of what I have now, I had to get the mind frame first. I had to get alone with myself a lot and see what God was telling me. By far, this is interesting, amazing, and shocking, the turn around my life has had over a short period of time. So like I said, it's critical that time must be used wisely but boldly toward what you feel you are to become in the kingdom of God.

Time is not a tool. Time can either work against you or for you. I know you've heard it many times before, but timing is everything. Start to develop you, so when the timing is right, you can step into it without a doubt. Know when traveling this journey, you will meet some people and you will outgrow some people. We are not grass or trees, meaning we are not born to stay in the same place and move side to side. When we were children and got old enough to move to our own place, we left because we outgrew our parents' home. *We grow into a mature adult the way we feel, the way we feel, the way we feel we are supposed to.*

Notice I said that more than one time because it's highly important to bring the way you feel to fruition. No more shall you act as a malfunction in life. Understand you are important to your feeling, the ones you love, and the people you have not met yet. You becoming a functioning person leads to life satisfaction. You want peace? Plant your good to reap good. You want true happiness? Let go of the things you worry about that you can't do anything about. Apply what you feel to feel the glory of God. If something feels good while you are thinking about it, put it out to the world so you can feel better that you tried something you thought about.

Every single person on this earth wants to be important and feel needed. Don't cheat yourself of your importance. So what if you lack the education? No one starts at the top. Remember, greatness is a process; it doesn't allow you to miss steps. Now I know I've been going for a while but to start a thing and keep it going is a tough job. I encourage you to open your mind to possibilities of success, opportunity, and growth. You will find a better lifestyle, greater feeling, and a better mentality. You are designed for greatness; expect nothing less from yourself, family, and friends.

From this day forward, talk the good talk. Speak uplifting words toward where you are going, and head in the direction to that future place. The battle is great, so you can become great. The battle is deadly, so you can become deadly. The battle can be conquered, so you can become a conqueror. Stop waiting until the perfect time. Time will never be perfect until you start. No, you will not always have all the money you want to start nor the people you picture will be here. The thing you see has to be built or created.

In the motion of building, money comes and also people. Understand many may not stay long or forever. God sends people to help and learn what they need from you. So therefore, it's always been his design for us not to stay in one place too long because it stunts the growth of a person. Always keep good gratitude because you never know who you are speaking with nor around could be your ticket. To finish a thing, go back and read this book again. I started it, and it took time, patience, commitment, determination, self-motivation, compassion, and many, many, many talks with God to finish. You carry what you got through the storms of life all the way to the end. Many people are thinkers and many are doers. A lot of thinkers can't do it because they do much thinking. Doers sometimes get a lot done, but is it what they need to do? We all have the ability to do both, but some people often lack one of the two.

When you want to become something, you must work both. Practice doing what you say. Practice meeting goals and deadlines. The moment you become a thinker and a doer, you become unstoppable. Think you can do a thing? Then do the thing you think you can do. When you start to do the thing, don't let up, don't give up, and don't stop until you did everything you could to make it happen. You've got what it takes to finish as well as what it takes to start. If you plan to do anything, map it out and start to finish.

ABOUT THE AUTHOR

....

Emanuel Jones is a millennial anachronism. Hailing from Memphis, Tennessee, he has held numerous jobs and started several businesses. As an over-the-road truck driver, he found himself with plenty of alone time to communicate with God. As he began to listen, God began to dictate a divine download. This book is a reflection of that download.

CPSIA information can be obtained
at www.ICGtesting.com
Printed in the USA
JSHW041334090722
27781JS00004B/12